Love in a Time of Loneliness

THREE ESSAYS ON DRIVE AND DESIRE

For R.R.

Love in a Time of Loneliness

THREE ESSAYS ON DRIVE AND DESIRE

Paul Verhaeghe

Translated by Plym Peters
and Tony Langham

KARNAC

First published in Dutch by Acco, Leuven, Belgium as
Liefde in tijden van eenzaamheid:
drie verhandelingen over drift en verlangen

English translation by Plym Peters and Tony Langham
Published by Rebus Press in 1999

This paperback edition published in 2011 by
Karnac Books Ltd
118 Finchley Road
London NW3 5HT

British Library Cataloguing in Publication Data
A C.I.P. for this book is available from the British Library

ISBN: 978-1-85575-698-4

Printed in Great Britain
www.karnacbooks.com

Contents

Prologue: Sex, Death and Power

There is no activity in which people make such efforts to achieve 'it' as they do in sex. The fact that this 'it' is never achieved, and cannot even be defined, doesn't inhibit this passion. On the contrary . . .

Every time I visit the British Museum it is a sensuous experience. As I walk through the different galleries and see the history of our forebears before me in tangible form, I try to imagine what life must have been like then, how Lindow man experienced death, what were the dreams of the Egyptian couple lying hand-in-hand carved in stone, how . . . and so on. But I can't do it. It must have been so different that it is hardly possible to imagine. Huizinga's *The Waning of the Middle Ages*, one of the classic works about history, is a classic precisely because it describes this different way of being so convincingly.

And yet there is a clear connection. The people looking at us through these works that lie in the museum display cases were motivated by the same things as we are, or there simply wouldn't have been any display cases. One of my best friends has summarised this very succinctly: it is always about death and sex.

In one way or another, all human culture is related to these aspects of human experience. It has been said before: the human being became human at the moment he first made a grave and buried another person. For me, the Venus of Willendorf is just as important, though this is about the other aspect, that of life and Eros in contrast with that of death, Thanatos.

In every museum of cultural history there is a third theme that is possibly even more clearly present: the theme of power. The question is whether this can actually be seen as a separate issue. Isn't power always an attempt to control the different aspect, the intangible, incomprehensible aspect contained in the first two themes? With regard to death, this is clearly the case: the wish to survive beyond death is the single most easily identifiable sign of power. With regard to sexuality, this is less obvious, and the link with power is much more difficult to expose. Moreover, sexuality is not simply linked to power, it is a cross-roads where power and death come together as a way of transcending death.

This power is situated between the two different types of people, between men and women. History has shown the direction that this takes: power, often brute force, wielded by men against women. Every society develops a system of rules for the division of power and desire. In the West, the balance of this division of power is also clear. The three 'nations of the book'—Jews, Christians and Muslims—have each in their own way banished the woman, together with eroticism, to a sort of limbo. The fact that both women and eroticism are finally managing to escape from this in gradual stages has all sorts of consequences. The first and most important consequence is confusion and doubt in men, as well as aggression and flight, and an attempt to return to earlier times.

Sexuality and death, linked through power, form a single element. A visit to the museum also leads to another discovery: for one reason or another it is precisely this triple image that has always been depicted, represented and symbolised from the very beginning of history. One of the first symbols is the monument of the tomb, and present erotic graffiti are not actually so very different from those dating from the stone age.

It is this representation and the need for its expression that link us with our predecessors in distant times. The emotion I feel when I see the small, usually pregnant, faceless figures of women dating from 20,000 years ago, is the same emotion I feel when I see Henry Moore's statue in St Paul's Cathedral of a stone mother and child that are two separate figures, despite their single abstract form. Beyond this emotion, there is some reflection, and this produces a difference. No matter how far Moore's mother and child are fused together, they can be seen as two separate entities standing opposite each other in a clearly represented, almost physically tangible, force-field. This separation is absent in the primitive figures in which the mother contains and incorporates the child. There were no separate representations of mother and children until very late in human history. The earliest known work at the moment is to be found in the Belgrade National Museum. It dates from 4,500 BC and depicts a bear goddess holding a bear cub in her arms . . . Strange . . .

All this has been present since man's infancy, and it is also present in our own infancy. Nowadays this has a special appeal because of modern life: the relationship between men and women is no longer self-evident, the function of the father is everywhere in question, and a number of certainties have disappeared. In this book my intention is to reflect on a number of timeless questions by looking at the form they take in our own time. How can we understand the relations between death, eroticism and power? What is the relationship between symbol formation and the resulting forms of expression and is it possible to discover an evolution over time here? Why is it that again and again it is woman who is the centre of attention? Why is there such a necessary link between passion and law? And, finally, what is love?

These are the questions that formed my starting point.

Acknowledgements

I'd like to thank Plym Peters and Tony Langham (Devon), my translators who did a marvellous job; Susan Fairfield (Cambridge, Mass.), my American editor who introduced me to the 'small differences' between European and American culture; Kirsty Hall (London), for our joint enjoyable close reading of the draft, even at six o'clock on a cold Innsbruck morning; Judith Feher (Boston), for telling me not to try to be too easy and to stick to my usual style (in other words, the first forty pages were so bad they needed rewriting); Parveen Adams (London), who made me revise the section on the collapse of the father function three times; and John Brenkman (New York), who added his unique form of humour.

Laarne (Belgium), Spring 1998
New York/London, Summer 1999

PAUL VERHAEGHE

(e-mail: Paul.Verhaeghe@rug.ac.be)

I. The Impossible Couple

The Divorce Express (by Paul Danzinger)
Mom's House, Dad's House (by Ricci Isolina)
Ellen is Home Alone (by Francine Pascal)
Jessie's Baby-Sitter (by Martin)
A Man for Mother (by Charles Nöstlinger)
Mum, Why Don't You Fall in Love? (by A. Steinwart)
Two Father, Two Mothers (by R. De Nennie)

Titles of recent children's books
(For children aged 9-12)

Spring 1969: Peter *Easy Rider* Fonda speeds on his bike through the American landscape, looking for freedom, leaving *Pleasantville* far behind. The sky is the limit. Autumn 1997: the same Peter Fonda plays a fifty-year old Vietnam vet, taking care of his grandchildren—his son is in jail, his daughter-in-law is a junkie and one of his worries is keeping his granddaughter off the street (*Ulee's Gold*).

Between these two movies, a world has disappeared that can be epitomised by the ubiquitous use of quotation marks—the 'lady of the house' invited the husband of her 'best friend' to her flat 'to have a drink'. Today, nothing means what it once meant. The perception of this cultural earthquake can be very different, ranging from an anxious plea for the return of law and order to a jubilant expectation of a new society. Independently of these moral interpretations, one thing is crystal clear to everyone: family life has changed drastically, the couple of yesterday has almost vanished and paradoxically (at least in most

Western European countries) the main defenders of marriage are to be found in the gay community.

So the very idea of a couple has, to put it mildly, become problematic. A 'couple' here means both hetero- and homosexual ones and is not merely a knee-jerk reaction to political correctness.[1] Old-fashioned declarations of romantic love—if they are still heard—sound rather hollow. The former expectations of undying love no longer apply; it is 'just for a little while', 'so long as it lasts'. The younger generation rarely uses expressions such as 'my love', let alone 'my husband/wife'—it has to be 'my partner'. Their parents' generation is often disillusioned, with many unfulfilled expectations. We will soon see the *Brave New World* effect, in which the cynic views the long-term loving relationship not only as an impossibility, but even as something suspect, as a sign of psychological ill health for which the two deviants have to be treated as quickly as possible.

At the same time, this kind of life-long loving relationship is still what both young and old are dreaming of. The failure to achieve it in reality serves only to make the dream even more vivid, as well as intensifying the search for new ways to achieve it. There has been a very clear change in emphasis: while the main thing used to be sex, the emphasis is now on security. Love is a remedy in a time of loneliness.

And a remedy is called for. One of the best legacies of imperialism is the discovery that a relationship between the two sexes always develops on the basis of a culturally determined set of rules. Every ethnic grouping has its own traditions, interwoven with faith and history, and this is what determines the nature of the couple. Following this discovery, it is easy to take the next step. In our own western culture, faith and tradition have been shattered, so that

2

the rules that were still determined by these factors yester-day have now disappeared. For the generation of our great-grandparents, the paths they had to follow were very clearly outlined: monogamous marriage, 'till death us do part'. The priest, the doctor and the schoolteacher all proclaimed the same message, and there was no room for doubt. Thus, every couple had to manage as well as they could within clearly defined limits.

These limits were removed in the second half of the twentieth century. The Wall came tumbling down and freedom was the new message. Freedom was to lead to a new and enlightened relationship between men and women, and it was expected that science would give it a new meaning. Certainly science has taken over the role of religion and ideology, both of which gave a meaning to life in the past. Men in black have been replaced by men in white coats. Initially this was accompanied by high expectations and the creation of a new sort of person. But there were no real answers, and today the things we learn from the laboratory sound less and less convincing. The result is that modern couples are desperately seeking a new for-mula that will tell them how to love. *Scientology* does have a future.

This search gives rise to all sorts of caricatured situa-tions, and it is particularly striking that liberating and enlightened science can provide as many compelling solu-tions as religion did in the past. This always happens in the same way: the research results start to serve as com-pulsory norms. When apparently 'scientific' statistics in a journal are published on how often an average couple 'does it' per week, this is enough for discussions to start in the bedroom: 'Look, we're doing it too often/not often enough'. A well-known women's magazine came to the conclusion, following a survey of 'our female readers', that, on average, the readers spent thirty-three minutes a week having sex, of which eighteen minutes were spent on foreplay and fifteen on actual intercourse. I can just imagine the quarrels between couples following this publication, in some cases combined with secretly timing their own performance . . .

The same thing happens in the name of serious science. In this respect, the best example is that of Masters and Johnson, whose scientific research also led to 'prescriptive' behaviour when their discoveries became norms with which sexual behaviour had to comply. Their pioneering investigation into physical sexual response patterns in the 1960s is still essential reading in that field. For example, they discovered that although men and women are comparable as regards their physiological and sexual responses, there are still two important differences. First, the woman can potentially have multiple orgasms and reach a climax several times while making love; in contrast, a man ejaculates once when he reaches orgasm. Second, the curve of the sexual response cycle is approximately the same for all men (arousal, ejaculation, temporary impotence), but is fairly varied in women. In other words, men are boring, monotonous creatures, and women are not. In fact, women discovered this for themselves a long time ago: 'All men are the same'.

The prescriptive behaviour begins when these discoveries are linked to a curious development in the emancipation movement. In a number of cases the feminists' demands for equal rights were translated into a demand for equality between men and women. If a woman has to be the same as a man, this also means that she must do better than him. Very soon, women were forced to follow the male pattern of love-making, with scoring orgasms as the central element. In the name of science, she was forced to take on the model of multiple orgasms that every man dreams of. What *can* be achieved *must* be achieved.

On top of all this, during the 'flower power' period, the orgasms of both the man and the woman had to take place at the same time if possible, with the result that the post-Masters and Johnson couple eventually turned into a couple where the man was desperately trying *not* to reach a climax, while, at the same time, the woman was equally desperately trying *to* reach a climax. It had been completely forgotten that the woman—despite her potential for having multiple orgasms—has a very different attitude to climaxing compared to the man. The male preoccupation with the actual phallus is in stark contrast with the lack of importance attributed to this work of art by the average woman. This was noted by Oscar Wilde, who said that the obligatory honeymoon trip of those times to the Niagara Falls was the bride's *second* great disappointment. The elliptical formulation he used is perfect because it effortlessly evokes a truth that is almost inexpressible.

At the end of this millennium, the initial euphoria about 'the scientific answer' has now faded and has been replaced with insecurity. There is another clarion call for new values and for a new security; these same values and security will probably be next year's new establishment. So we will have to hurry to ask questions before a new morality makes them superfluous. The most pressing question is about the need for this sort of context. Why should there necessarily be any culturally determined rules for something that was once thought of as being a 'simply' biological act, namely, sexual activity?

The concerned techno-lover

This was certainly one of the convictions that became popular during the sexual revolution. Sexuality and eroticism are simply natural activities and nothing more. Education and culture were no longer allowed to put obstacles in the way. Children left to grow up in freedom would spontaneously discover their own sexual pleasure and would be able to develop their adult sexuality with the same freedom of feeling. It was even thought that they would develop erotic activity in a playful way and refine it to an art, in contrast with the uptight, bedtime sex of their parents. This aspect of sex as a game has a number of characteristics that it shares with an itch: when someone's back itches and a willing partner is prepared to scratch, he/she hardly ever finds exactly the right spot where it itches most, and it's really difficult to explain where this spot is . . . It's something that you should really do yourself, but that doesn't work either.

Seen in this light, sex is a matter of technique, which, of course, reminds us of the old complaint by feminists: there are no frigid women, only useless men. The Dutch sexologist Paul Vennix produced the following apt formula: since most women climax with oral or manual stimulation, then consequently the main forms of sexual dysfunction in men—from the perspective of a female-oriented sexology—will be an aching tongue and stiff fingers. Nowadays the average man is trained as a techno-lover, with all sorts of video sex education, computer applications and so on. In the event of being undersized—and the fear of this is never far removed—there are now more than enough technical aids available. But what is the result of all this? When modern man tries to use all the tricks he has carefully acquired in practice—the 'foreplay' that was so important at one stage—he is often given the lowest mark for his effort. Now that he can do it, it is no longer required. I'm reminded of a well-known anecdote by Lucien Israel, who was treating a non-orgasmic woman when he started to practise as an analyst. The analysis was going fairly well. In fact, it went so well that at a certain point the woman told him she had made love to her husband and that she actually had an orgasm. After this, she brought the happy analyst down to earth by adding: 'And now I don't want to make love to him any more'. She desired something that she didn't want.

There is more to all this than just technique. Reducing it to a technical aspect was a typical male product of sexual liberation, in which sex was nothing more than a need situated between the navel and the knee, from arousal to orgasm. Soon this was converted into a performance model, where scoring was the main goal. It was at the same time that the myth of erogenous zones arose: find the right spot and stimulate it in the right way, and 'arousal' is presumed to follow automatically. Hordes of men went in search of the famous G-spot, and actual training sessions were organised, with massage, pressure techniques and so on. In short, this was a version of the prenatal yoga class and even therapists themselves saw Masters and Johnson's sex therapy as a sort of elevated form of keep-fit. Eventually it took a woman, Helen Kaplan, to add to this so-called two stage model (arousal/orgasm), the essential third stage, desire. But 'stage' is the wrong word, since desire is more of a pre-condition: without it erogenous zones are of no importance whatever. In fact, when there is no desire, they become a source of disgust. *Inter faeces et urinam nascimur.* 'We are born between faeces and urine'. When there is desire, everything becomes erogenous. In the first instance the reduction to a 'Mr Fixit' model typi-

7

fies the male approach, it is no coincidence that the majority of women haven't a clue about technique and assiduously attend evening classes on 'DIY for single women'.

Beyond this male preoccupation with and female lack of interest in technique, we can see what all this represents: unspoken expectations that provide support and guidance, giving men an idea of what women want, and vice versa. In other words, the underlying fantasy.

Fantasies that create reality

Attention to the practical aspects of sex reveals a characteristic element of the male imagination, particularly the focus of attention on the body and on certain parts of the female anatomy. The converse hardly ever applies. This difference can be illustrated in a physical way: a striptease by a woman for a male audience is not the same thing as a striptease by a man for a female audience. When there are male spectators, the tension is tangible, and at best there is an almost sacred silence. On the other hand, when the Chippendales—once a word synonymous with beautifully made furniture—perform their act, the women laugh themselves silly, and it is easy to think they are actually laughing at the men.

There is another curious phenomenon: the average man is easily misled/seduced by a transvestite, another man playing a woman. *The Crying Game* (Neil Jordan) and *M. Butterfly* (David Cronenberg) are exceptional films only because of the actual story, not because of the seduction itself. On the contrary: the red light district in every metropolis has a significant number of transvestite prostitutes whose clients are constantly being misled. I am reminded of a scene from an American detective writer

(Patricia Cornwell? Walter Mosley?) where the hard-nosed cop quizzes the traditional rookie when they are driving past kerb-crawlers in the red light district. How do you recognise the transvestites? 'They're the ones with perfect tits and legs'. Thus transvestites display super-female characteristics even more perfectly: a super-female *from the perspective of male fantasy*. There are few women who are as 'feminine' as transvestites. By analogy, it could be said that a relationship between two women is usually much more satisfying for the women involved and does not need a transvestite!

The success of these relationships has nothing to do with the fact that a partner of the same sex has a more suitable technique or knows where to find the right spot. It is somewhat naïve to think this. The success is mainly due to the fact that within these relationships the similarities between the respective fantasies of the participants are much greater. The male transvestite playing/embodying a woman does so on the basis of his male fantasy of the ideal woman; that is ideal for another man. The emphasis is on the so-called super-feminine aspect, in other words, the physical aspect. For women matters are a little more difficult. A woman who seduces another woman does not embody the ideal man, or does so only to a very slight extent; rather she embodies something beyond external appearances, something like an ideal relationship or ideal love. That is why there is no need for transvestism here. The distinction is even stronger in homosexual couples. For male partners, 'scoring' is the thing; for female partners, 'nesting' prevails.[2]

Meanwhile, we have found a really useful definition for a man and a woman: one is a fantasy for the other. There is a Parisian story about a masked ball. A secret couple finally see an opportunity for spending an evening together—after all, everyone is wearing a mask. They make an arrangement for an intimate rendezvous afterwards. During the party they flutter around each other, and when the clock finally strikes midnight they hasten to the rendezvous and remove their masks. Then they find: 'Alas, it wasn't him, and it wasn't her, either'. Each of us approaches the other person on the basis of our own fantasy and sees the other primarily as no more than this fantasy made real. When couples come together, there is a meeting of two fantasies that initially seem to fulfil each other—though the correspondence is rarely perfect: 'It wasn't him, it wasn't her, either.'

Why do we have fantasies anyway? Fantasy—the representation, staging or detailed spinning out of a story—is undoubtedly one of the most essential components of eroticism. Without it, the erotic element is reduced to the animal level and is not even erotic anymore. With fantasies, it becomes human. Moreover, these fantasies cannot be limited to individual daydreams. They also form the basis of every kind of art. As Freud wrote in his article on 'Creative Writers and Day-Dreaming', the artist successfully expresses his own fantasies in such a way that others can also enjoy them, with the ultimate intention of acquiring power and erotic allure. This brings us back once again to one of the questions in our introduction: why is there this ubiquitous need for imagination?

It would still be premature to answer this question now. Let us begin by looking for a moment at the difference between the two types of fantasies. Is there such a thing as a typically male fantasy, or a typically female fantasy? We can find an answer when we look at the way the different sexes fantasise. This is one of the most delicate of subjects, perhaps the most concealed and suppressed of all. There is little scientific research and when questionnaires *are* used they are generally not very reliable. The two things people lie most about are sex and money. However, there is another source of research which is readily available: the commercial expression of our imagination.

For men, these images are easy to find, since pornography is a typically male product. It is an open secret that video libraries get most of their income from renting adult-rated films, and these are mostly taken out by men. The women shown in these videos are always the same. The short-skirted, big-bosomed (silicone!) secretary/nurse who seduces her boss/doctor within a very short time. She is not only challengingly desirable, she is also immediately sexually available. In fact, she wants only one thing, here and now, preferably as long and as often as possible. In other words, she is the perfect projection of his fantasy. Male sex is visual and genitally-phallically oriented with a clear goal, orgasm. After that, it is time to get up and go.

For women, these images are not nearly so obvious. There is hardly any female visual pornography as a counterpart to male pornography, and where it is found it is a subsidiary phenomenon of a particular form of feminism. Literary erotic stories 'by women for women' that have recently appeared on the market so controversially are read just as much—and possibly more—by men. I suspect they are often even produced by men. Even Anaïs Nin was commissioned to write them for a living, but she wrote them for a man and adapted her stories to his taste. To find the real female counterpart we have to look for something radically different, something quite separate from the male fantasy. Once this is understood, it is fairly easy to find what you are looking for, because it is for sale at the same newsagents. The books for women are right next to male pornography; kitchen-sink drama, Harlequin and Mills and Boon romance and the like. In spite of feminist indignation, world-wide sales of these are mind-boggling, and any writer of 'literature' will be green with envy. The stories produced in these books are just as stereotyped as their male counterparts, though the emphasis is completely different. A thirty-something woman with an unhappy love affair behind her goes to work as an au pair for a film director (doctor, company executive etc) whose wife has just died. She looks after his two small children. Despite their initial dislike, she falls in love with him, but unfortunately he is in love with a film star who is merely using him to get on in her career. After many misunderstandings they discover that they love each other, etc.

The female eroticism in these stories has hardly any visual content, is never genitally focused and has no clear goal. It takes place in a timeless interval. The man is the central element in the woman's fantasy and is always very special, not because of his looks, but because of his position. There are some constant elements in all the different versions of this romance. He is not bound by a current love, and tends to be withdrawn. He has to be won over. Usually he does not at first understand that she, the other protagonist, is his true love, but as soon as he falls in love with her he will do everything he can to make sure this love lasts forever. This always leads to all sorts of difficulties and that is what the book is about. In so far as there is any sex, it is only part of the story, but never the main part.

This sort of man is the perfect projection of what a woman wants herself, just as the randy, sex-crazed woman mentioned above was the perfect projection of the man's desires. Consequently, these two fantasies are not mutually exchangeable. A woman doesn't understand what her man 'sees' in pornography: it's always the same thing. A man doesn't understand what his wife finds in these stories: it's always the same thing. In extreme cases, this ends with typically sex-linked perversions—fetishism in men and erotomania in women. Fetishism means that the man's libido is increased by what at first sight merely looks like accessories, with lingerie, boots and high heels being the most familiar, though in fact any object can serve as a fetish. A closer examination shows what these accessories mainly do is reveal the man's fear of what is 'different' in a woman, and the fetish serves as a sort of lightning conductor in this respect. Erotomania means that a woman stays in love with an inaccessible man through thick and thin, hoping that he will return this love in the same way, and even feeling convinced of this. Nothing can persuade her that this is not the case, and the victim sometimes has to call the police and go to court to deal with her.

The question is whether these two phenomena can still be seen as perversions. Fetishism is so widespread in the average man that it is often perceived as normal behaviour, and women will indeed go to great lengths to maintain a relationship.

Of course, there is no such thing as the average man. Apart from focusing on his phallic performance, every man dreams of a loving and lasting relationship. The average woman doesn't exist either and the erotic fantasies of many women go much farther than their partners would suspect. Nevertheless, one is a fantasy for the other, and the two are not always attuned. For the man, the phallic sexual act is a goal in itself. This explains the complaint often heard from women: 'he only wants to have sex, there's never any time for talking or tenderness'. For women, this phallic sexual act is more of a means for achieving a different end, namely establishing or maintaining the relationship. This explains the complaint often heard from men: once a relationship has become more or less established, the woman is no longer very interested in sex. When the relationship is threatened for one reason or another, she suddenly becomes interested again.

Clearly, we are in deep trouble.

Self-fulfilling prophecies

The man expresses his desire mainly in sexuality focused on the sexual act; the woman does this much less and has different and more varied forms of expression. The result of this difference is that there is a snowball effect resulting in a self-fulfilling prophecy. After all, the mere fact that the average man is always ready for sex has a devastating influence on the desire of the average woman. When chocolate is always available and even forced on you, who wants chocolate?[i]

On the basis of this omnipresent male pressure, the man hardly hears the woman's 'Yes, I want you too,' and sometimes she hardly hears it herself. 'How can I ever feel

---

[i] In defence of chocolate, one of the last products to be exported from Belgium, I would like to put forward the following top twenty reasons 'why chocolate is better than sex', taken from the Internet:

1. With chocolate, size doesn't matter.
2. Chocolate satisfies, even when it has gone soft.
3. 'If you love me, you will swallow that,' has real meaning with chocolate.
4. You can safely have chocolate when you're driving.
5. You can make chocolate last as long as you want it to.
6. You can have chocolate even in front of your mother.
7. If you bite the nuts too hard, the chocolate won't mind.
8. Two people of the same sex can have chocolate without being called nasty names.

14

like sex, I hardly get the chance, he's always waiting ...'
What is heard all the more clearly is her response 'No, I
don't feel like it *now*.' The result is that increasingly men
start to look for sex away from home. Nowadays, this is
not so difficult to find, and because of the way things are,
the other partner will also be looking for a new relationship. This means that the erotic aspect is also a central element for the woman at that moment, though mainly as a
means of forging a new relationship. She is meeting a new
man who will not be moving quite so quickly, since it is the
f st time, and who therefore gives her a chance to feel her
own desires. Success is guaranteed. The result of all this is
that the man becomes convinced that he has found a
woman who is looking for phallic and erotic sex just like
him. He is even more convinced that his wife at home is
really rather 'frigid'. Meanwhile, the chances are that the
so-called 'frigid' wife is actually no longer at home at all,
but in some exotic little restaurant where she is building
up a new passionate relationship with a new partner who
has had enough of *his* frigid wife at home and so . . .

This is pure vaudeville, a caricature transcended only
by reality. The tragic version can be found in the non-

9. The word 'commitment' doesn't scare off chocolate.

10. You can have chocolate on top of your desk without upsetting your co-workers.

11. You can ask a stranger for chocolate without getting your face slapped.

12. You don't get hairs in your mouth with chocolate.

13. With chocolate, there's no need to fake it.

14. Chocolate doesn't make you pregnant.

15. You can have chocolate at any time of the month.

16. Good chocolate is easy to find.

17. You can have as many kinds of chocolate as you can handle.

18. You are never too young or too old for chocolate.

19. When you have chocolate it doesn't keep your neighbours awake.

20. You can GET chocolate.

emancipated layers of society, where the betrayed wife stays at home like a good girl and finally discovers that her husband has been unfaithful. Actually, most men help her find this out in order to assuage their constant feelings of guilt. At this point it is by no means unusual for the man to cite her sexual coldness as a reason for his escapade, the ultimate proof being that the other woman 'really wants' him. The 'good wife' may even believe this and feel inadequate as a woman. After all, a 'real' woman wants to make love all the time doesn't she? Almost every women's magazine includes at least one article in every issue about perfecting the erotic desires of the modern woman ('Tantric sex goes deeper!'), the delights of a holiday romance ('If he ever found out!'), the quality of orgasm at a mature age ('Never too old to experiment!'), love affairs in the nursing home ('Ssshhh! the nurse is doing her rounds!'). If she didn't go along with this, she would feel very old-fashioned and abnormal, excluded from a sisterhood to which she clearly doesn't belong.

The opposite type of emancipation—in which the woman has to be equal to the man and even exceed him in every respect, including the phallic orgasmic competition—eventually results in a new form of female suppression: the woman is acceptable only when she appears in men's clothes, until this finally become a caricature. Who was the man who said of Margaret Thatcher, 'She's the man I always wanted to be?' This leaves no room for the woman to discover her own female desires.

Therefore it is not surprising that the drives become the ultimate divisive element in the relationship between men and women. This is one of the reasons why among heterosexual people friendships develop much more easily between men or between women than between men and women. In the latter case, the erotic drive is always present, and while this can be a source of the physical development of a friendship in a number of cases, as a rule it merely leads to difficulties. This has a well-known side effect: women often get on best and have long-term friendships with homosexual men, because the sexual drive is absent from this relationship. The woman does not feel threatened or obliged to please, the man does not have to seduce her, so it becomes possible for them to really come together without feeling forced to.

What about biology?

At first sight, what was described above looks like an explanation for the failure of the heterosexual relationship: the man and the woman have completely different desires starting from different fantasies—in John Money's terms, they each have a different 'love map'. The remedy is a psychological compromise and appropriate counselling aimed at achieving mutual understanding. This is the deal—sex in exchange for a solid and tender relationship, and vice versa. It may not actually be put in such crude terms, but that is what it really amounts to. Every psychotherapist with a few years' experience can tell you the same story. Right from the start, the man wants more sex than the woman. The result is that it becomes more and more of a chore for her and less and less of a pleasure, with familiar consequences. For women, this leads to faking orgasms (young woman), headaches (slightly older), refusal (mature). For men, there is insistence, cajoling, moodiness, drinking, and ultimately the traditional ways out: restarting masturbation (in so far as this ever stopped), a lover (preferably ten years younger), or paid sex (for those with the money to get it). The main sex education that Queen Victoria gave her daughter was: 'Lie back and think of England'. Of course, there are other possibilities, as in the case of Anthony Burgess's Italian girlfriend, who said, 'It gives you so much pleasure and me so little bother, so …'

Whatever the case may be, there is a difference. For many people this situation is a sufficient argument for assuming that polygamy is more in line with human nature than monogamy. In this context, references are inevitably made to one or the other species of apes where the privileged males always lord it over a troop of females. The confusing thing about this is that with these 'proofs' taken from ethology, it is possible to prove anything, depending on the sort of ape that is chosen. Whenever I pick up these studies I can never escape the impression, reading between the lines, that the 'objective' male or female researcher is trying to justify his or her own sexual behaviour by modelling it on the 'proven' promiscuous or monogamous behaviour of some monkey. Poor creature.

The problem that arises here is related not so much to biology or genes as to a typical characteristic of this male-female relationship, particularly the demand for exclusivity. We will explore the origin of this later. The same reasoning can be turned into one of the most powerful arguments for the influence of culture. After all, this supposedly polygamous natural-man theory works only in so far as it is supported by a sympathetic culture. Preferably this should go back for several millennia, and the older woman should be given a different, but every bit as exclusive a role as the younger woman. Traditionally, she is given a position of power and wisdom, while the younger woman has to make do with bed and birth. In cases where polygamy is not supported by a cultural tradition, it is a guaranteed source of misery. For me, this is a sufficient proof of the supremacy of culture over nature.

However, science has little interest in those aspects of culture that cannot be quantified. For scientists, everything must be weighed and counted so that all is clear. The constant production of male sperm means that men are continually following their penises, while women who produce only one egg every month are much more difficult to get going. On the basis of this neo-Darwinist approach, many scientists try to convince us of the fact that we too are merely blind reproductive machines with only one goal: to produce a new generation. Taken to its logical conclusion, even this use of the word 'we' is dubious, because according to the scientists, it is quite apparent that it is the genes who do the 'wanting'. Leaving aside the teleological/theological impasse—who does the wanting and who wants anything to be wanted—this gives rise to intellectual gymnastics culminating in the ultimate answer to the most existential question: what is a human being? It is the way in which genes reproduce.

Thus, little by little, sexuality has been reduced by these scientists to a small playing field—the same one as the Catholic Church restricted it to—reproduction. If we are no more than a collection of genes focused on reproduction, then it is obvious how the difference between men and women can be explained. *Naturally*, men are promiscuous, because the more women they fertilise, the greater the chance that their genes will be multiplied. *Naturally*, women are more focused on monogamy. After all, in contrast with the unlimited production of male sperm, they can produce only a limited number of descendants, so they opt: a) for the highest achievable man, who is b) prepared to help with the rearing of the joint gene production.

Putting this even more simply, from the neo-Darwinian point of view the man invests in quantity, the woman in quality.

Scenes from a marriage (1):
'Yes, I know that I've betrayed you again, and yes, it was with a much younger woman, but what can I do, it's my genes and I can't help it, can I?'

Scenes from a marriage (2):
'Yes, it's very difficult for you to realise that your son is not yours, but after all, my boss is simply much more intelligent and my genes realised this even more quickly than I did, so it was out of my hands, wasn't it?'

In both cases the high priest of neo-Darwinian science will grant absolution and allow each partner to 'go in peace'. But the battle goes on.

What this argument has failed to take into account is that people—and now I am *not* talking merely about collections of genes—have been consciously looking for an efficient method of 'family planning' for centuries. Until recently, this amounted in virtually every case to birth control. The majority of promiscuous men are certainly not out to get their girlfriends pregnant—on the contrary. Something isn't right.

What is wrong with these reductive biological models is precisely their reductionism: it is true that we are collections of genes, but we are not just collections of genes. Probably we are the only collection of genes that also has an element of choice, no matter how limited this is. This choice can oppose whatever it was that was inscribed in the original biological programme, because a new and different software has developed which has started to play a serious role. This software is called culture. It evolved from nature but has now transcended it. Neo-Darwinian fundamentalists will see this as scientific heresy and reject it with a shrug of the shoulders. Then they will join their medieval predecessors with their own version of the doctrine of predestination: everything is determined, free choice is inconceivable, we are blindly driven on by an equally blind watchmaker.

This demonstrates the fact that the very idea of free choice is threatening, extremely threatening. Most of us are usually prepared to pass on the choice as quickly as possible, to God, to science, or to the advertising industry. There is absolutely no doubt that we are organisms with biological drives, and that the drives of thousands of years echo in our genes. However, it is equally true that we can decide what we do with these genes, and hence, we are also responsible for these decisions and accountable for the consequences. Culture is actually a collective decision in which rules are presented and imposed. Every new generation tries to modify it, and ultimately every individual can break away from this culture if he/she is prepared to pay the price. The minimum price for this freedom is always the same: loneliness, which is much less fun.

Divided desire

No matter how attractive sociobiological and evolutionary explanations of the differences between men and women may sound, they are not enough. It is not that they are untrue. Far from it, but they only scratch the surface. What is wrong with these explanations soon becomes clear when we look at the converse argument. What happens when a normal man, that is, a man who wants immediate sex, runs into a female version of the same thing, a woman who also wants to dive into bed straightaway, anywhere and everywhere? The chances are that the man will quickly lose interest and even take flight—in this case, with his non-proverbial tail between his legs. In the context of the psychoanalytical situation, I have often seen this happen with male analysands when the apparently biologically set roles were simply reversed. It was by no means unusual for the man to complain that he felt used and even abused, reduced to an object, a vibrator. In other words, he voiced exactly the same complaint as a woman would. Men are so afraid of female desire and pleasure that they have even created a scientific term for this, 'nymphomania'. This is ultimately no more than the scientific expression of the mythology of the *vagina dentata* (the vagina with teeth). The opposite proof can be constructed for the woman who is expected to have little or no desire for sex. What happens when she is coupled with a man whose greatest interest is in platonic discussions on the usefulness of reed beds for the ecological purification of waste water? Either she drags him into the reed beds with her, or she will take a lover.

Once again, we find what we touched upon briefly before: a desire for something that is not wanted. There is an *internal* division in desire. This is a difficult idea to grasp. Surely desire is straightforward and at most inhibited by external factors? Freud initially used this argument. Thus, patients actually became patients because they were sexually frustrated: their desires were inhibited by external prohibition, usually imposed by the family or society. It is no coincidence that one of his early texts carried the following message in the title: '"Civilized" Sexual

Morality and Modern Nervous Illness'. Removing this double morality and the accompanying prohibitions, in combination with some internal modification, would, he hoped, open the golden road to absolute pleasure. However, Freud soon discovered that his neurotic patients were frightened of this. In fact, they created barriers to prevent themselves from achieving satisfaction. All games need rules; rules to act as a restriction, though this does not prevent people from complaining about them in retrospect. Lacan formulated this laconically: 'The desire of an hysteric is to have an unsatisfied desire', and we should not forget that for him hysteria is synonymous with normality.

This internal division is not immediately visible, because people usually succeed in externalising it. They attribute this division to another person and then complain about it. Whom does a man fall in love with? With a woman who refuses him, who plays hard to get, who never wholly gives in. Whom do women fall in love with? With the unattainable man of whom they can only dream, but who never, etc. We predicted above what would happen in the converse case: the internal divisions become fully apparent and the person ends up being completely confused.

This is a curious phenomenon. Just at the moment when someone is wanted, desired by another, the chances are that he/she will run a mile. This is odd, because everyone wants to be desired, and yet it is exactly what people complain about: 'He doesn't want me, he just wants my body', 'She doesn't want me, she just pretends, she just wants my money'. So why do people run a mile at the point when someone else clearly wants them? Closer consideration reveals that this happens mainly when infatuation reduces us to the *passive* object of the other person's desire. For some reason, this reduction is a threat to both men and women. It means that, apart from the above-mentioned differences between men and women as regards their fantasies, there is also a fundamental similarity which overrides gender. Everyone wants to be loved, but at the same time everyone finds it intolerable to be reduced to the passive object of the other's desire. The traditional distribution of sexual roles was divided along the lines of the active desire of the man and the passive rejection of the woman, but nowadays this situation can easily be reversed. The same reasoning applies to homosexual couples. Clearly, we need to look further.

The difference between male and female fantasies is not sufficient to explain the dissatisfaction between men and women. There is obviously an internal conflict at work, independent of any issue about gender. We can even end up reversing the traditional scenarios. The man who is out to have sex may take flight, while the cool diva may turn into a nuclear power station going into meltdown. We want what we do not desire, and we desire what we do not want. It seems as though our very desires contain an unwished for element so that we are confused rather than pleased if we satisfy them.

This brings us to a strange phenomenon: feelings of guilt in victims of sexual crimes. Although this is well-known, it is not adequately accounted for in the often simplistic approach to these matters. It simply does not fit with the black and white picture of the undivided ego where the baddies always wear black and the goodies always march in white. The position of some radical feminists that always puts the blame on the man has as its mirror image the equally unsubtle macho reproach that she was 'simply asking for it'. Consequently, the idea that the development of feelings of guilt in the victim is a way of coping with fear—since feelings of impotence are much worse than feelings of guilt—is never understood. Similarly the distinction is not made between *active dreaming* of the passive position and being forced to *undergo passively* what was dreamed. In my third essay I will return to the relationship between activity and passivity and to the idea that fantasies are a way of coping with the trauma of the passive position.

The question about the reasons for the difficulties in sexual relationships concerns the problem of the internal division between pleasure and desire. This internal division was the starting point for Freud's work and throughout his life he attempted to formulate it in several ways. The best known examples are the contrast between the conscious and the unconscious, and, later, the division between the ego, the id and the superego. However, his theory contains many more discussions of this division. There is even one that is directly applicable to what was described above: the contrast between what he calls the affectionate and the sensual aspects in people. It should be noted that he is referring to people in general and is not dividing them neatly into men and women. In his work *Three Essays on the Theory of Sexuality*, Freud links the success of a person's love life to the way in which he/she succeeds in resolving this contradiction.

> A normal sexual life is only assured by an exact convergence of the two currents directed towards the sexual object and the sexual aim, the affectionate current and the sensual one. It is like the completion of a tunnel that has been driven through a hill from both directions. (Freud 1905b: 207)

Continuing the same metaphor, it seems that in many cases the tunnel is never finished. And even where the work is finished, you often end up with two tunnels, that is, two relationships, one for the affectionate aspect and one for sensuality.

This is certainly an everyday clinical experience: tenderness gets in the way of sensuality, and vice versa. It is the rule rather than the exception for small children who happen to come across their parents making love—the so called primal scene—to interpret this as a fight. Too much tenderness on the part of the man does not really do much for his erection, and a tender wife cannot really expect much hard sex from her man—let alone ask for it—because it is not the done thing. This difficult combination can also be understood as the continually problematic marriage between the sexual drive and love, so that we will have to go in search of a practical definition of each. What is this drive? What is love?

Animal instincts, human drives

We shall start with what Freud calls the border area between the body and the psyche. This border area is the drive. For a while it was fashionable to reduce the sexual drive to something rather like an instinct. Sex was seen merely as an instinct, a need like any other—eating, drinking, sleeping—and all the moralising was superfluous. Strachey's translation of Freud gave the German 'Trieb' as 'instinct'. This leads to all sorts of difficulties at the rare moments when Freud refers to 'instinct' as such. It is no coincidence that he makes a distinction between drives and instincts. On the contrary, a study of the instinctive mating behaviour of animals in ethology makes it possible to measure the distance that divides us from animals. In this respect, the ethological X-rated classical example is the unsurpassable stickleback. In the spring, the male develops his mating colours and makes a nest at the bottom of the pond. When he sees another male, he promptly attacks. In contrast, he will start a loving mating dance when he sees a female and they will eventually mate.

Described in this way it all seems very idyllic, and we might well be jealous. It even reflects an ideal of emancipation, because it is the male who is responsible for the nest and looks after the spawn. It all seems rather less idyllic when we see that the stickleback attacks not only his male rivals, but anything that is red and torpedo-shaped, and that he not only dances for the female but around any silvery cylindrical object that enters his field of vision. He even desperately tries to mate with it. The shining knight we saw just now is merely a blindly driven reproductive machine. The mating behaviour of the stickleback is wholly determined by an organically directed system of body markings. The male does not 'see' an attractive female but responds to the markings of a swollen silvery object. He does not 'see' a rival, but a red torpedo, and attacks this and only this. The whole mating ritual is strictly determined within certain limits on the basis of heredity and imprinting. If the markings are changed too much, it all fails. Within the limits of these markings this characteristic behaviour is repeated again and again.

In sticklebacks, and in a wider sense in all animals, there is a sexual relationship in the sense of a predetermined pattern of behaviour for the mating ritual. Whether this involves any pleasure is an open question that is suggestive of anthropomorphism—our incorrigible tendency to want to recognise ourselves in everything, always and everywhere. On the other hand, the human drive is not an instinct, but rather a mutation of a number of originally instinctive responses. The original sucking reflex of a baby soon changes into something else, sometimes into something so different that it counteracts the original survival function, with anorexia and bulimia as the most obvious examples. This completely removes the idea of reflexes and instincts as determining elements in human beings. In order to survive as a subject, the body is sometimes almost sacrificed, either by starving it or by exploding it. *The Hunger Artist* by Franz Kafka reveals a great deal more insight in this respect than many current bio-psychological theories. I know that I am leaving the reader with some questions here, but art cannot be explained. Anyone with anorexic tendencies will understand.

Drives: partial and auto-erotic

As I remarked above, the original meaning of a drive is a concept see-sawing between psychological and bodily aspects. For Freud, it comprises four components: the source and the pressure, on the one hand, and the aim and the object, on the other hand. The first two have a physical basis, and the second two a psychological basis. This seems almost intuitively understandable in the sense that the source lies in the body, a presumed combination of sexual organs, genes and hormones that together result in the pressure, a sort of energy tension level. In this naïve naturalistic view, the aim becomes the sexual act, and the object is 'obviously' someone of the other sex. The whole thing is presumed to be orchestrated by psychologically caused reflex patterns in which all sorts of fixations and conditioning will have entered during childhood. From Pavlovian saliva to Pavlovian erections. Why not?

No matter how attractive this view may sound, it is incorrect, not least because of the fact that it ignores two fundamental characteristics. The first and probably most important characteristic is that every drive or impulse is always a *partial* impulse. The second characteristic, one that immediately follows on from the first, is its *auto-erotic* nature. Consequently a drive, as such, is originally neither hetero- nor homosexual.

What do we mean when we say a drive is partial? This should be interpreted in the light of an implicit—and therefore unspoken—expectation about what is a 'normal' sexual relationship. The basic idea in this expectation is that there is 'something'—a drive, an instinct?—that drives them together for sex and reproduction. A closer study of this 'something' soon reveals the opposite phenomenon: the 'something' driving the two people together consists of a number of separate components that are brought together only in retrospect. This reveals itself first of all in the development of childhood sexuality, when these different aspects—the oral, anal, urethral aspects—appear in a random fashion. The same constituents can easily be identified in adult sexuality, when the classical bungling of the famous 'first time' in itself serves as an argument for the lack of any reproductive drive.

Therefore a drive has only a partial contribution to make in connection with the sexual act itself. In concrete terms, this means that there may be such a thing as an oral drive, an anal drive, a voyeuristic drive, and so forth, in human beings, but there is never an 'overall' sexual drive that drives the male (genitalia) inexorably on to the female (genitalia). Lacan later developed this Freudian discovery and formulated it as: 'There is no such thing as a sexual relationship.'

A very specific consequence of this characteristic is that the drive never works on the whole body but is always focused on fragments or on individual activities. The drive does not need a whole body; it is always one particular part of the body that is involved, together with an activity related to this, which can be either active or passive. These parts of the body are always the points of interaction with the outside world: the genitalia, anus, mouth, eye, ear and nose, together with the related activities of smelling, listening, looking, sucking, penetrating.

There is a great temptation to simplify the catalogue of the different types and subcategories of drives, conceivable combinations, and so on. After all, we have always been taught to 'go and name things', and the odd word of Latin and Greek also sounds very scientific. By analogy with the categories of manias (kleptomania, pyromania . . .) and phobias (agoraphobia, claustrophobia, hydrophobia . . .) it would be possible to draw up a summary of drives (oral, anal, scopic . . .) together with their deviant forms. In the past, these were known as perversions; nowadays we use the term 'paraphilias' (don't say 'pesticide', say 'phyto-pharmaceutical product'). The lists drawn up by Money in this respect leave a great deal to the imagination, with ambitious terms such as apotemnophilia (paraphilia which involves erotic gratification from amputations of one's own body), acrotomophilia (the same thing, but in reverse: the amputation is carried out on the partner), peodeiktophilia (have a guess). Borges' *Book of Imaginary Beings* is as nothing in comparison.

Carrying a system to an extreme always reveals the internal errors. A catalogue of drives is impossible because everyone develops their own variations. The only thing that survives in this argument is the fact that 'the' drive is always partial, partial in relation to a presumed goal that is ultimately never achieved. These partial drives are laboriously brought together during the course of development under so-called 'genital primacy', but this is not very convincing. A clinical expression of this can be found in the fact that each of us, despite reaching genital adulthood, has his or her own erotic preference beyond strictly genital activity.

Thus the first central fact is the partial nature of this drive. The second essential characteristic of the impulse concerns the object. An impulse is not only focused on parts of the body and the related activities. In the first instance, it also concerns a person's *own* body, and it is only at a later stage that the body of another person becomes involved. In other words, the drive is essentially an *auto-erotic* matter. It might be thought that this auto-erotic aspect is age-related and comes to an end with the arrival of another person as a partner, but this is not the case. The auto-erotic aspect continues to be an essential aspect of the drive even when the actual sexual activity is apparently focused on another person. From the point of view of the partial drive, this other person is always a means, and he/she never becomes a goal in him/herself. In pragmatic terms, this suggests that the drive does not require a person as a subject in any way. The movement of the partial impulse is that of an arc, a boomerang, that passes over the other person, returns to itself, and closes in on itself, creating a totality, a completed action, self-gratification. The basic model of this is the infant's mouth, which closes around its own thumb as the infant falls asleep, quite content and separate from the world. Unfortunately, it soon finds that it cannot survive without this world, and in particular that it needs other people if only, in the first instance, to achieve this self-gratification once again.

Therefore the goal of the partial drive is not the other person, the goal is to achieve a particular form of gratification. In this respect, the other person is actually superfluous as a subject and can sometimes even be an obstacle to pleasure. He or she serves as an object—and actually as a *partial* object—a means of achieving a goal.

There are several reasons why this theory is rather repellent. It is clearly the most rejected aspect of Freud's work. The fact that the sex life of people amounts to a mere collection of partial impulses, partial in respect to both the goal and the object, may be just barely acceptable. However, the fact that these partial impulses are, and continue to be, essentially masturbatory is hard to take. The other person is always reduced to an object that can be exchanged. I will return later to the question of why this auto-erotic element is rejected, the most well-known consequence being, in the past at least, the universal prohibition on masturbation.

This sort of description of the drive leads to a suspicion that ultimately every human being could be described as being perverse. Freud does not go this far, but he does describe the child as a 'polymorphously perverse being', by which he means that the seeds of all possible later adult perversions can be identified in childhood. When you look at your own memories, you will soon discover the games of doctors and nurses that you enjoyed playing as a child with other children, games in which many of these partial drives were explored in detail. They involve looking at— and, of course, showing—the urethral, anal and genital areas and also include aspects of domination and being dominated. They apply to children both of the same and of the opposite sex. When you come across one of these former playmates from childhood by coincidence—at a school reunion, a large family gathering—the same inner question arises in both partners: 'Does he/she still remember that?' They certainly do! The next step is the observation that these children's games, together with the accompanying childhood fantasies, can clearly still have an influence on adult sexuality.

The discovery that the seeds of different types of deviant sexual behaviour are present in all of us allows us to turn a particular question around. If one assumes that the sexual relationship is determined by biology, the question then is how does someone *become* perverse? In other words, why is it that someone will deviate from what is assumed to be biologically determined? This presupposes that a perversion is a tendency 'against nature'. On the other hand, if we work on the basis of the idea that we all start with a strange combination of partial drives, a very different question arises: why is it that we have not all *remained* perverse? In some way, the majority of us go through some sort of normalisation process when we are children, so that these original perverse tendencies are sufficiently modified. In this light, the question can be formulated in even more specific operational terms: why is it that these partial drives become more or less brought together and subordinated to the strictly genital sex act per se? Moreover, why is it that this collection of partial drives is then focused on another person as the love object?

This normalisation process is the so-called Oedipus complex. I hesitate to use this term, because it seems so well known that everyone is immediately ready to give their own caricatured definition. For the time being, let me describe it as follows: the Oedipus complex is the process through which everyone has to go in order to move from two to three elements, that is, to break away from a mirror relationship with another person who is the same, and take the step towards a third person, another other.

Love is ...

This brings us, after the drive, to the other end of the tunnel—love. It is often thought that what was described above with regard to partial drives is the basis for a psychoanalytic debasement of love. There has been a reaction against those Freudians who considered it necessary to describe all elevated feelings in infantile terms of shit, piss and the like. I should like to slow down these hasty critics, because, up to now, I have not yet said anything about love as such. The most obvious difference between a drive and love concerns the object, which should no longer be referred to as an object. In contrast with the drive where the object can always be exchanged as an unimportant means to an end, in the case of love, everything turns upon this one irreplaceable other. There is barely any room left for the self, and the loved one takes up all the space available. As Freud says: 'A person in love is humble.' This is not only a difference; it even indicates a direct contrast. How can these two aspects be reconciled?

Freud writes about love, and so does Lacan. In itself, this is unusual, because the subject of love does not really seem appropriate for a scientific discourse. In the human sciences the emphasis should at least be on relationships: 'disturbed relationships', 'communication problems', 'sexual dysfunctions' and so on. In the hard scientific world, the idea of love is viewed as a poetic and therefore half-baked description of something that must ultimately be reduced to conditions based on hormones and genes. Thus Freud's interest was all the more remarkable, particularly because he studied love as a separate issue, alongside, and independent of, the drives. It was something different, but what? Trying to define it is almost an impossibility. Both Freud and Lacan make a distinction between being in love and love. Freud sees being in love as related to hypnosis, being under a spell. Lacan introduces a neologism, *'L'hainamoration'*—*haine, amour, admiration,* (hatred, love, admiration)—to describe the narcissistic aspects of being in love. 'Mirror, mirror on the wall, who is the fairest of them all?'—we love and hate ourselves in the reflection of the other, and the strongest aphrodisiac is someone declaring his/her love for us.

Beyond the state of being in love, there may be real love, but the problem of definition remains. It seems to be a universal phenomenon, yet we have had to invent poetry to say anything meaningful about it. It is true that the most penetrating pages on this so very human phenomenon have been written not by scientists, but in what is known as the arts, the field beyond science. And would there be music without passion?

A closer study and a reading of Denis de Rougemont shows that perhaps this traditional view should be taken with a pinch of salt. Love, as we now know it, is actually a very recent phenomenon, and it also has a geographical limitation. The definition is familiar to us in terms of the exclusive relationship between a man and a woman, in which the exclusive aspect is that one person has to be more or less everything to the other person and vice versa, a relationship that usually produces children who then have a place within the relationship. In other words, this is what is popularly known as 'the nuclear family'. Our western arrogance is such that we have imagined for a long time that this is the only true form that has always existed in some form or another and will always continue to exist, from the Flintstones, through the Cosby family, to the Jetsons. Historically this relationship is a fairly recent development, and it is restricted to certain population groups. It will be argued that before our times there were also marriages and love affairs. This is true, but not in the modern sense of the word. We should not forget that marriage was and is primarily an *economic* matter focused on the division of property and on inheritance; that is why marriage and the property-owning classes go hand in hand. The have-nots do not and did not need it. Marriage in the first half of the twentieth century was a co-production by Hollywood and the Vatican, that has undergone significant changes, though the economic basis still survives. For example, this is perfectly expressed in the current need for 'cohabitation contracts', which are no more than a modern version of a marriage certificate, and in particular an arrangement about how goods should be divided. In this respect, a marriage between homosexuals is perfectly conceivable and understandable.

Does this mean that love is also merely a recent invention and that the idea of eternal love is no more than a fantasy? It certainly does not, for in psychoanalytic terms, love is literally at the basis of existence itself—it just happens that we do not find the prototype in the relationship between men and women, but elsewhere. The basic model of love should be sought not in the relationship between a man and a woman, but in the *relationship between mother and child:* this is a love of all time. However, this does not mean that it has not evolved.[3] In the second essay, I will show that the Freudian Oedipus complex is in itself a part of this evolution. I have found the starting point for this in the primitive figures of pregnant mothers. It is continuing to evolve today, and because of this, the concept of what constitutes a mother, child, father, man or woman has changed.

Meanwhile, we have formulated one of the most important Freudian insights: that the very first human relationship provides the template upon which all later relationships will be based. This is known as transference. It does not mean that these later relationships have to be a faithful copy. They can, for example, be the precise opposite, but this does not remove the determining character. On the contrary, as Kierkegaard wrote: 'Repetition is a beloved wife of whom one never tires'.[4] This sentence is misunderstood by almost everyone. On the basis of this misunderstanding, it is either confirmed (by those who are happily married) or criticised (by those who are happily divorced). When you read the expression, it is easy to interpret it as follows: 'The beloved wife/husband is a repetition of whom one never tires.' However, for Freud and Kierkegaard, the *repetition* is central, the repetition on the basis of which a partner is ascribed a particular place, and not vice versa. At the same time, repetition then had a different meaning. Nowadays, repetition has become almost synonymous with boredom. One only has to think of a children's game that is endlessly repeated and yet gives pleasure every time, in contrast with the blasé adult who always wants something new, something different, something that might still rouse him from the lethargy of excess.

Thus, to say anything meaningful about love, we have to look at the primary relationship between mother and child as it is found in its twentieth-century manifestation, particularly within the nuclear family. There are three general characteristics of this relationship: first, this form of love is total and exclusive; second, from the very beginning, it will inevitably fail to survive, and leaves a feeling of loss which gives rise to desire; third, it is characterised by power.

. . . total and exclusive

Initially, the relationship is total and exclusive. At first, there is nothing beyond it, the one is everything to the other, and vice versa. The mother and child 'unit', as it is described today, actually is a 'unit', a single entity with little or no room for anything or anyone else. In describing the mother and child as a unit, this applies to a far greater extent than one might think. For example, it means that mother and child simply do not exist as separate entities. This clearly undermines the idea of a 'relationship'. Rather than a relationship between two individuals, there is a fullness, an absence of anything lacking. This is actually the case during pregnancy. It is striking that the period of pregnancy is described by the majority of women, once it has come to an end, as a condition of unparalleled well-being. To describe this situation, Lacan used the term *jouissance*, which has all sorts of layers of meaning. In the first place, it means pleasure. In the French language, the word also has a legal meaning, in the sense of the profit arising from the use of something that belongs to someone else. In this way, the subtleties of language create what at first sight seems a curious link between pleasure and usufruct. The child is the fruit of the body and it is clearly a source of pleasure.

This physical—and therefore real—unity during pregnancy continues to exist for a while afterwards in an imaginary sense during the postnatal period, revealing a fullness, a sensation of being enclosed. Outsiders are outsiders by definition. The figure who feels this most acutely is the father: every brand-new father has to convince himself that he is a father, despite what he feels. He has lost his wife—she has become a mother—and he is shut out of a relationship that he cannot understand. Paradoxically, he will become a father only at the moment when the child can acknowledge him: 'The child is father of the man'.

It is in this early relationship that the ground is laid for something that will lead to all sorts of difficulties later on—the demand for exclusivity. 'Mummy's boy, the most beautiful child in the world' and 'My mum is the best ... ' are only weak expressions of this exclusivity, which cannot be overestimated. The other person is *everything* to me, and *only* to me, and any third figure is automatically a threat. This demand for the exclusion of everyone else normally comes from the child, particularly when there is a rival in the form of a new brother or sister. From that moment, there is a struggle for exclusive attention and love ('His orange juice is bigger than mine!'), the source of all subsequent jealousy, envy and resentment. This also explains the special position of children who grew up as only children without brothers or sisters, particularly sons, who really did have an exclusive relationship with their mother. There is a great danger that these children will become tyrannical egoists later on in adulthood, always expecting others to do their bidding. We are now presented with a large-scale involuntary experiment in the largest population group in the world, namely, in China. As a result of the official birth-control policy, there is almost a whole generation growing up there with no brothers or sisters, so that they are assured of such exclusive attention.

The effect of this cannot be predicted, but there is no doubt that it will have an effect.

This same demand for exclusive attention can also exist on the part of the mother who finds it difficult or impossible to tolerate the fact that the child, her child, should devote any attention to others. 'Miss is *so* nice' is not always a popular remark. When there is already some rivalry between a woman and her mother-in-law over the husband/son, they will inevitably shift the battle to the child/grandchild. The one wants to be the one and only one.

The most familiar consequence of this demand for exclusivity in the child is the adult demand for unconditional loyalty. The threat posed by a third person is just as intolerable as the attention of the parent for another child, who therefore automatically becomes a rival. All attempts to have 'open marriages' prove how stubborn this demand continues to be, and demonstrate the fact that the average mental age in this respect is not much more than five years old, that is, the Oedipal period. So I do not interpret monogamy as a biologically determined characteristic but as an effect of the original dual relationship between mother and child. However, this certainly does not make it any the less compelling.

. . . *cause of lack and desire*

In its original form, this all-encompassing relationship is doomed to disappear along with its exclusivity. We are left with a fundamental sense of something lacking, as well as with an insatiable desire. Aristophanes' classic fable in Plato's *Symposium* describes the same desire, though giving its own explanation. According to the fable, the human being was originally always a dual figure, either a double male, or a double female, or a hermaphrodite with a double gender; each had a double back and chest, four hands, four legs and two faces on the same head, looking in opposite directions. The story goes that this original being was so conceited and powerful that Zeus felt compelled to divide it in two. Since then, we have all spent our lives looking for our lost other halves.[5]

The psychoanalytic version of this story is much more prosaic—instead of a mythical double creature, we start from the undifferentiated unit of the mother and child. This unit is also divided in two, which results in the creation of desire. In this respect, a particular error of interpretation often occurs. It is thought that the child 'loses' its mother. It then goes in search of this original mother, so that every subsequent partner is compared to this original partner who satisfied every desire. This is only partially correct. What the child loses is not the mother, but the relationship with the mother as a *unit*, that is, the condition of preverbal symbiosis. This also explains a curious phenomenon—even the mother, the so-called 'original' love object, is no longer good enough either. This can be observed from early childhood. When a toddler asks for a drink at bedtime, it expresses this need by pestering its mother. If there were a perfect correspondence between the request for a drink and the need, it would be enough simply to give the child a drink, but anyone who has ever had children knows that this is never the case. The child asks for a drink and expresses an unquenchable desire in his request, a desire for something else, for something different. After the drink, he wants a pee, and then he feels hungry, and so on. Clearly he wants his mother to stay with him, but even that is not enough. She doesn't just have to be there, she

41

has to be *all* there, completely for him and for him alone, in a way that cannot in reality be achieved.

Through this demand for her to be present, the child is really asking for something else, something that can apparently never be put into words. I heard this expressed most clearly by a toddler—how could it be otherwise? 'Mum, I wish you were a toadstool, then I could live in you.' The child longs for the preverbal unity that was first broken at the time of birth, a break which must be repeated, and above all, consolidated, in and by language. The-mother-and-child unit is definitively lost, because language comes between the mother and child. That is where the real loss occurs, or more accurately, the loss of reality of things, by the introduction of the symbolic, of words. Before language, there is immediacy without mediation, and the child's needs operate automatically. Afterwards there is a gap that can never be bridged.

An animal without language is part and parcel of its reality. It has no chance of the self-reflection or distance that we achieve through language. After the introduction of language, distance and mediation follow, and therefore difference. This applies first and foremost with regard to the other person who really has become an 'other', the (m)other, but it equally applies to oneself, since this is how an identity is created that can be reflected upon in terms of language. 'I think, therefore I am' demonstrates this distance. Rimbaud expressed it much more poetically: 'Je est un autre' (I is someone else). It is said that language is a bridge, but it is a bridge that at the same time creates the chasm it bridges, and what lies under the bridge is lost.

Language is not so much a means of communication, as it is a means of achieving *identity*. Through language, every person acquires a certain identity, with related rules: you are the mother of, daughter of, father of, son of. Thus the original real division of birth is symbolically consolidated within the Oedipal structure, where everyone is assigned their rightful place through words. At this point we become human, leaving nature behind for good. The rest of this dividing operation is nothing other than desire. It is also the explanation of the continually shifting nature of desire. You 'desire' something from another person, either something vague or something specific, but it is never enough, and you continue to desire, beyond this something, the other person's self, but when this other person gives himself, even that doesn't really satisfy . . . So what is it you really want? What you really want is the sense of unity that has been lost forever, the enjoyment of the totality that once existed. This is what keeps people going initially in the primary relationship with the mother and later on in all other relationships.

The art of saying no

This brings us to the third characteristic of this first love relationship: that of power. The original relationship is an omnipotent one, in the sense that each half of the unit is effectively everything to the other. When this unity is broken, this *all*-powerful attribute changes into power, and this is accompanied by a transition from the verb *to be* to the verb *to have*. While the two halves of the relationship initially complete each other within a unit, after the division this changes into a pattern of give and take, and therefore possibly a *refusal* to give or take. Think of an eighteen-month-old baby, crying for his mummy all weekend long. When she finally comes back, he turns his head away and doesn't want to look at her.

Give and take, asking and refusing, all this presupposes that there is 'something' that is asked for/can be given, something that could meet the other half's needs and wants. This is the basis for every form of gift or exchange. It is also here that each of us learns to give and take in our own particular way, to such an extent that it often becomes a typical personality trait. How does someone give or respond to a gift? How does someone ask for things, even if only to ask the way, or does he/she always want to do it on his/her own? In other words, how does a person deal with a desire? In this context, the loss that the need represents has to be interpreted both in a literal way (Where are my keys?) and in a very allusive way ('*Weltschmerz*', 'soul searching', 'the blues'). The loss is of something that the person does not have but wants to have, or is something he/she is not, but wishes to be.

In this first loving relationship this . giving/taking/refusal initially manifests itself in so-called pregenital development. This term is used to describe those parts of the body that play an erotic role in the adult without being part of a narrow genital register. The best known are the oral and anal zones. There is a development of this pregenital aspect: a child learns to eat and to speak (the oral), to pee and to shit (the anal-urethral). This is based on a number of physical maturation processes. However, the purely organic development of the body is by no means sufficient to explain the nature of this evolution. The typical aspect of pregenital development is that it takes place in an *interaction* between the child and the request of the other. It is the other person (the mother, and many other people in her wake) who *asks* the child to eat, burp, sleep, shit, talk, look and listen at regular times—*her* times. This interaction seems to take place continually between mother and child, with the mother constantly making demands on the body of the child, and especially at the points of interaction between its body and the outside world.

The importance of all this cannot be overstated. After all, it is in and through this interaction that the partial drives start to play a role, and the drive assumes its place between the child and other people before any gender involvement. Prior to this time, the drives operated autonomously, but from now on others become involved. The result is that, henceforward, love and drives develop jointly as part of the broader development of the child into adulthood.

Every child therapist knows that the interaction between the demands of the mother and the developing child has a very decisive effect on development. This is most apparent when there are no demands, because this means that little 'development' is taking place. For example, it is well known that some parents of Down's Syndrome babies continue to have expectations and hopes of development for their children. These children then achieve a much more 'normal' development than those whose parents have no such expectations. Normal babies of whom little demand is made, because their parents have very few expectations, are very likely to remain underdeveloped. Children who grow up with parents who make pathological demands always retain the scars. It is impossible to predict what the precise effects will be, because the child is not simply a passive entity to be moulded, but an active and interactive human being with its own unpredictable contribution to make.

The child responds to the demands made by others and makes choices: he/she can refuse to eat, can eat everything, can refuse to speak, can refuse potty training. 'Why is it that he's perfectly dry at school while things always go wrong at home—it almost looks as if he's doing it on purpose'. Expressions in the vernacular provide an answer: He is 'pissed off' with other people and the demands that are made. In adult, that is, in genital love, this giving/taking/refusal manifests itself with regard to a very sensitive issue, namely, orgasm: who gives whom an orgasm? Who refuses to have an orgasm? Raymond of the Groenewoud pop group sang about this, 'Girls, you can't get them to come, man'. Sometimes intercourse can be almost like a fight, where the man wants to give the woman pleasure because he has/gives the phallus and is convinced that the woman's desire is for that phallus. The fact that a number of women kindly fake an orgasm is a willing gesture that soon shows who's boss.

Normally this power lies with the mother, the *alma mater*, which begs for a retranslation of the well-known adage: '*Ce que femme veut, Dieu le veut*'(God wants what a woman wants) as '*Ce que maman veut, Dieu le veut*' (God wants what mother wants'). This is also an appropriate place to bring up man's 'innate' fear of woman. The shadow of the mother falls on every woman so that she shares in the power, and even in the omnipotence, of the mother.

This is every young policeman's nightmare: a middle-aged woman rolls down her car window and asks, 'What is it, son?'

It is this original omnipotence that evokes fear in all its aspects, from sexism to misogyny.

About boys and girls

It is in the nature of things for this initial omnipotence to be shattered: the mother is not always there, and even

46

when she is present, she is not there in the same way as she was before the division. She is never enough, she is not what the child had hoped for. When the child turns to the father, after a while he is disillusioned there too. The father is not the hero of his dreams who will come up with the perfect solution for every problem. Almost every adult will have some painful memory of the moment when he/she discovered that their parents did not meet the ideal that they had gradually built up. The discovery of the mother's shortcomings reflects the child's discovery of his own failures and shortcomings. Whatever he does, no matter how he tries, and even if does his best, he will never be able to meet the mother's desires perfectly, just as she will never again experience the sense of completeness that once existed. One of the cries most often heard from children is: 'It's not my fault', which in itself shows to what extent the child is struggling with blame and fault, and hence with failure. There is a Dostoyevsky in each of us.

After the mother's omnipotence is destroyed and this sense of shortcoming is established, there is a search for something beyond, outside the original dual relationship, something that can complete this lack, something or someone who can produce a solution for this loss. In the classical Freudian view, this is the point when the father appears as the person on whom the mother's desire is focused beyond the child, the father as the bearer of the phallus. After this period, the development of the child divides into that of the girl or that of the boy. On the basis of anatomical considerations, they will adopt a different position vis-à-vis this lack.

In western patriarchal society, the little boy soon assumes that the solution to the lack in his relationship with his mother, lies in the man/father and the latter's genital organ, and his own little willy also promises to become 'big and strong' one day. Of course, there is always the danger that this promise will not be fulfilled or will be inadequately fulfilled. The fear of not complying with this norm, the norm posed by this apparently enormous father, has two consequences. On the one hand, the man always feels the need to prove himself: the 'Guinness Book of Records' hysteria is a typical male disorder. On the other hand, there is the development of an archaic extremely strong superego, easily interpreted as the conscience, and a related sense of guilt as a reaction to the fear of this original giant father who was seen as a rival.

Thus, this *norm*-al man is both phallocentrically and authority-oriented. He also assumes that this applies to women. However, the development of the girl takes a different direction. The first difference is that the boy, as a future man, can retain his first love object in terms of gender; he merely has to exchange it for another woman. This explains the curious fact that, after a while, many men adopt the same attitude to their wife as they originally had to their mother. In contrast, the girl has to change the gender of her love object. More specifically, she has to exchange her first love object, the mother, for her father. As a result of the first loving relationship, she still identifies with the mother and therefore hopes that she will be given the same love by the father as he gives to the mother. This explains the equally curious fact that many women become like their own mother once they have become a wife, and above all a mother, themselves.

The most important effect of this change with regard to the object is that the girl will pay much more attention to the relationship itself, in contrast with the male preoccupation with the phallic aspect. The girl's lack of interest in the object and in the phallic aspect, and her emphasis on the relationship, may have the result that in later life her relationships do not have to be with a man. After all, her original object was also of the same gender, and during puberty the first love is almost always for another girl.

In this light, the penis envy that Freud believed to be important in girls—the presumed desire of girls to have their own phallus—seems more a product of his own male, and consequently phallocentric, imagination. The only place where I have ever found this famous penis envy up to now is in men. It is based on their constant fear of inadequacy and their continual imaginary comparisons with other men's penises. The female counterpart of this male phallocentrism is a focus on relationships.

Another result is the fundamentally different attitude of women to the law, that is, to the original authority of the father. While a boy has every reason to be afraid of his father as a rival, this is not the case—or hardly applies—for a girl. On the contrary, he is the one who gives her love or should give her love. Therefore it is not surprising that women have a much more relaxed relationship with law and authority. This has led certain post-Freudian analysts to question whether a woman really has a superego—rather like certain mediaeval theologians who wondered whether women actually had a soul. A more practical and less esoteric result of this difference in terms of patriarchal Oedipal history is that men are much more susceptible to hierarchies and so much more likely to establish centrally led groups. The church and the army are men's groups. In contrast, women have a much less hierarchical tendency and organise themselves more horizontally, so that they form less of a group.

When we think about this kind of development, it soon becomes clear which is the weaker sex and where the power lies. As I will show, the patriarchal system and phallocentrism are merely pale reflections of an originally omnipotent matriarchal system (although the terms patriarchy and matriarchy here have slightly different meanings, see essay II). The implication of the development outlined above is that there are two sorts of love from the very beginning: a first all-embracing love that failed and was replaced by a second, far less satisfactory love. The first, pre-Oedipal form resembles jouissance, the second, Oedipal version is characterised by the less satisfactory dimension of desire. Once they are adults, both men and women will try to resolve the original failure and related narcissistic humiliation with their partner by trying to fulfil his/her desires, in this way returning to the original condition of wholeness. Everyone does this by focusing on what they themselves consider important, the man centring on the phallus and the woman centring on the relationship. The fact that this is precisely the opposite of what the partner considers important, means that a repetition of the original failure is in effect pre-programmed. It is only during a later, post-Oedipal version that something different, something new, can be started.

The power of the imagination

The first love has to be given up in its original form. In other words, every loving relationship has the seeds of failure within it, in so far as it expects a total return to a primordial state of unity. This failure is felt most strongly after the momentary fusion of the orgasm as a remaining phenomenon of the original symbiosis. The observation *'post coitum omne animal triste'* (after intercourse every animal is sad) is not a Freudian discovery. What *is* a Freudian discovery is the link with representation. According to Freud the child will try to restore the original symbiotic state of pleasure by hallucinating it, that is by representing and imagining it to him- or herself. The two diluted versions that survive in adults are dreams and fantasies, both known for their character of wish fulfilment.

There is something curious about this phenomenon of wish fulfilment. In dreams, it is rarely the case that the wish to be fulfilled is clear, and even in daydreams the actual fulfilment of the wish is a bonus. Yet, the wish-fulfilment character of both these processes is beyond dispute. 'Oh, I had such a wonderful dream last night.' 'What about?' 'I'm not quite sure.' So what does this wish fulfilment consist of? It is not a matter of completing 'the' act, whatever this may be, but a matter of its *representation*. It is a very special representation, quite different from symbolising in words (the latter being a process that always creates distance). The immediacy experienced in dream images is a distant echo of preverbal unity. We lose ourselves in the image, we *are* the image, and indeed this is the essence of the pleasure. The daytime counterpart of the night-time dream is the imagination. It is not known as 'daydreaming' for nothing. Again we are taken over by the imaginary aspect of its immediacy. It is a free ride to pleasure, beyond the divisive experience of 'I think, therefore I am.' Above all, it is a free ride that includes a return journey, as we shall see below.

Obviously the modern version of this is film, in which the viewer can lose himself to his heart's content. Is it possible to see the root of art, art as representation, in this wish to return to preverbal unity? Is it a coincidence that one of the oldest products of art consists precisely of representing this original unity, namely the primitive figures of pregnant mothers, of which 20,000-year-old examples have been found throughout Central Europe?

People desire unity with their beloved, a *unio mystica*. The blissful and direct images of dreams make us long to achieve these by day in real life, but the car still has to be taken to the car wash, the grass urgently needs mowing . . . Normal people don't get round to it, and only unusual and exceptional people succeed. A description of their experiences reveals that what is longed for so much is suddenly seen in a very different light. These accounts can be found in rather unexpected places, particularly in the works of the mystics: Hadewijch, St John of the Cross, even Pascal. Each of them does actually depict this unity, and the same characteristics constantly recur.

First, there is the direct presence of what is usually called 'God'; second, the mystic adopts a passive position in relation to this, and he/she cannot actively intervene; third, the experience cannot be spoken of or described. The whole experience is one of extreme pain and pleasure, with the recurring characteristic that the mystic ceases to have a sense of himself/herself, as an individual. Another description—or is it another interpretation?—can be found in the field of psychiatry. This condition of unity with the original environment, separate from any reflective distancing, is hallucinatory psychosis, daytime dreams from which it is difficult or impossible to awake. The main difference from the mystic is that in this case there is no sense of bliss. It is replaced by an almost indescribable fear.

This brings us to a second interpretation of the extremely difficult Lacanian concept of jouissance: that which the psychotic experiences at the acute moment of his psychosis, the moment at which he once again becomes one with the Other. A striking example can be found in the film *Shine*, where psychosis erupts at the moment when the protagonist finally completes the Other, namely, when the son wins the piano competition and by so doing fulfils his father's lack/desire. Scott Hicks makes us feel this by focusing on the reality of the situation. We no longer hear any music, just the dull sound of the furious hitting of the keys of the piano, we see and almost feel the perspiring face of the son—the next moment he has disappeared. He has disappeared in the sense that the person who was there before the psychotic eruption now no longer exists.

The price for completeness is very high. You pay for it with your own self, and you disappear as an individual. Jouissance: usufruct, the fruit of and for the Other.

Culture and the prohibition of incest

The complete fulfilment of desire and a return to the original symbiosis imply the disappearance of the subject. This sort of return is rather rare, because the primary bond of love is normally given up for good during early development. In traditional Freudian theory, the father is assigned the role of the divisive authoritarian. He is the one who is presumed to come between the mother and the child. This sort of role division conjures up archaic images—mother knitting by the fireside, father with his pipe and newspaper in the easy chair, the child being taken to bed at the right time. Before waving aside this idea as being a typical expression of an outdated phallocratic patriarchy, it is worthwhile exploring what this is based on, apart from the way in which it manifests itself as a product of a particular time. Lacan's reinterpretation of Freud on this point identifies the father with language. In nature, there are no fathers, there are only female animals with their nameless young, while cultures have mothers with children who are given names in order to express the way in which kinship relationships are structured. This relationship is always 'patriarchal', though this does not necessarily mean that it concerns the western nuclear family and the real father. The structure of relationships is patriarchal in the sense that it entails the *symbolic* recognition of a relationship, beyond the natural ties of the mother and child. The emphasis is entirely on this aspect of recognition. Even in those societies where the term 'fatherhood' is used in the narrow patriarchal sense of the word, biological fatherhood is never sufficient in itself. The man always has to acknowledge his fatherhood—it is no coincidence that the word *testes* is the root of *testimony*. It does not matter whether this form of relationship consists of the recognition by one father ('You are a Jones'), or on recognition by a totem group that may even be organised in a matriarchal system ('You are a kangaroo'). Something or someone must provide this recognition. The important point is that in being given a name, a child is referred to the third structure and in this way leaves the original dual bond.

Rereading the Oedipal structure in this way is very far from the traditional interpretation of a boy in love with his mother and afraid of his father, or of a girl in love with her father but afraid, etc. Rereading it in this way makes it possible to understand the current evolution taking place in society. I will return to this in the second essay, which deals explicitly with the historical evolution of the father's function.

At some point in history, the step from nature to culture that was taken in phylogenesis (the development of the species) is repeated in ontogenesis (the development of the individual). The original 'natural' love is lost, because it is forbidden by a universal prohibition. This is the familiar prohibition of incest. In fact, no matter how differently the relationships between the man, the woman and the child are arranged in different cultures, there is one recurring feature—this prohibition—focused on the symbiotic bond between mother and child.

This is the original interpretation of the prohibition of incest. The mother must surrender her product and let it go, and the child must leave the symbiotic bond. The current emphasis on incest between father and daughter means that this original meaning has been almost forgotten. The first meaning enables us to understand Oedipal desire much more accurately—more accurately than the caricatured interpretations that would have us believe that Johnny wants sex with his mum and Mary with her dad. What every child wants, whether it is a boy or a girl, is this pregenital natural unity with the first love object. What every culture actually prohibits is being enclosed with this first Other.

It is only during the second stage that the prohibition on incest also applies to the father as a third figure. Then it becomes a prohibition on *genital* incest. When the father ignores this prohibition and uses his child as a sexual object, there will always be some misunderstanding at first: the child does not understand the genital aspect and expects/hopes for something else, for something like the first love: 'Confusion of Tongues between Adults and the Child', as Ferenczi wrote. This form of incest is of a second order and always has severe traumatic effects. On the other hand, the original primary form has psychotic effects, and prevents the subject from acquiring an identity of his or her own.

As a result of the current wave of cases of incest, the emphasis is almost exclusively on this prohibition of incest as such, and its necessary counterpart, the injunction for exogamy, has been forgotten. In anthropological terms, this means the obligation to find a partner outside the family circle. It is the external formulation of a rule that goes far beyond this: every child must go 'elsewhere', and develop something and become someone there. This explains the necessary loss of the first relationship. The necessity of this loss can best be illustrated by those situations where it does *not* happen, where a perfect dual unity continues to exist, a perfectly closed relationship from which there is no exit. In clinical terms, this means that he or she is 'everything' for his or her mother, and that the person concerned does not lead their own life. Sometimes they hardly even have an identity of their own. This conjures up the image of a particular species of monstrous fish in the deep seas, in which the female is *n* times as big as the male. The male nestles on the female's back before mating in such a way that it literally becomes fused to the female, and from then on it merely becomes part of her.

It is a misunderstanding to think that this sort of phenomenon is restricted to the mother-child relationship. Potentially every love relationship contains this danger, in which the so-called 'strong personality' completely swallows up the weaker one. 'He/she has completely devoured her/him' is a popular way of describing it, which unconsciously—and therefore accurately—focuses on the primitive oral aspect of the first love.

In metaphorical terms, exogamy means that one has to leave the mother country to discover the world, certainly if one is to discover the 'dark continent'.[6] This brings us to the all-encompassing importance of love, because it means nothing less than that love and its manifestations form the basis for culture as a whole, in the widest sense of the word. In concrete terms, the implication is that we must all

56

lose our first love so that we can do everything we can to regain it, albeit 'elsewhere'. Culture develops in this movement and actually *is* this movement. There is absolutely no doubt that the human being is the most driven and most passionate creature ever to walk this earth—and the source of this passion is none other than this restless desire to rediscover 'it', while this 'it' can assume absolutely any form. On our way, we write poetry, listen to music, build cathedrals and fly to the planets. Paradise lost, paradise regained.

Masturbation and addiction

Now we are in a position to take another look at a subject that has already been touched upon and try to understand it better. This is the ever-present discomfort about masturbation and auto-eroticism, despite all the liberation slogans. 'Which part of the body is most intensely used while masturbating? The ear.' The fear of being caught at it, as well as feelings of guilt, are widespread, and continue to exist even after the sexual revolution. This shows that the guilt that is felt goes much further than arbitrary prohibitions, those determined by culture and family. This prohibition was quite far-reaching. For centuries, nearly every disease or abnormality was sooner or later attributed to onanism whether this was poor eyesight, a crooked back, tuberculosis, psychological problems or total insanity. Masturbation was once the great impossible subject in sex education: 'Idle hands do the devil's work', hands above the sheets, peepholes in boarding school dormitories, and the like. For those who persisted in this evil, all sorts of cruel mechanical devices were developed to banish the desire.

57

Originally, sex education did not really provide an explanation of reproduction and sexuality but tried to warn children and parents of the dangers of this unmentionable masturbation. Current youth education programmes are certainly no longer about sex, but focus the young people's attention on the dangers—and therefore attraction—of drugs. Both types of information have many similarities: they are provided by authorities on morality (the church, government, school), aimed at children and adolescents, and warn against a particular type of pleasure. There seems to be a strange link between the two.

As a result, the question seems to become all the more insistent—why is there is this prohibition on masturbation? 'What's the difference between masturbating and fucking?' 'Fucking—when you fuck, it's a social event, isn't it'. Masturbation is essentially auto-erotic, that is, you don't need anyone else, you rely on yourself and the original condition of omnipotence. Masturbation skirts round the rule on exogamy, the obligation to go to someone else, and in this sense it is incestuous. It is incestuous in the original meaning of the word: pleasure within a symbiotic relationship with another who is not distinct from oneself. It is a fantasised reinstallation of the conceited, self-satisfied beast with two backs, that finds pleasure on its own and consequently leaves everyone and everything else alone. The most despicable personality is the self-satisfied person who, in his arrogance, barely notices anyone else.

This explains the link with drugs and alcohol, where the user also finds other people superfluous and discovers the direct line to pleasure through these products. The main character in Trainspotting declares, 'Take the best orgasm you ever had, multiply it by a thousand, and you are still nowhere near it.' The addict opts for an 'economic' solution, saving himself the detour via the other person and all the problems and efforts that this entails. A whiz kid from the advertising world understood this perfectly when he thought of the following advertisement: first, we see a beautiful princess kissing a frog, and then the creature turns into the prince of her dreams; then we see the prince of her dreams kissing the princess, and she turns into a bottle of beer . . .

It is no coincidence that every society tries to control drink and drugs, because the uncontrolled, that is to say the non-ritualised use of drugs, places a person outside the group and outside the collective effort that is so necessary for the group's welfare. The drug addict finds his pleasure—and nothing else matters.

Love and drive—the tunnel

Masturbation has an incestuous element because it is able to do without another person and therefore seeks to make contact with the original auto-eroticism and the related sense of unity. On the other hand the presence of a partner, either in the imagination or in reality, does not necessarily imply that this incestuous aspect has been left behind. The bond that has been built up during the Oedipal period is such that its weight is inevitably carried along. This weight can be felt where the adult man/woman looks for a someone to build up their 'own' relationship: the word 'own' is between quotation marks because the choice of partner will always in some way be indebted to this original—and therefore incestuous—love. As one analyst said to another, 'Incest is fine as long as it is kept within the family'. We must all take our incest *outside* the family, which is difficult, doubly difficult.

First and foremost, many people have scores to settle with the first love objects, their mother and/or father, either on a credit level or on a debit level. Settling these scores takes place mainly in two fields: professionally, and in their love life. The fear of failure is not lodged in some part of the brain that is not functioning properly. One fails, just as one builds up a career, to please or to spite one's mother or father. The first words of a graduate who had just successfully gained his doctoral degree were: 'That's it, she's got her doctor now!' The next step is that the earlier score is settled with a subsequent partner, so that the shadow of the past falls over the present relationship like a lead weight. A woman who still has a score to settle with her father will be merciless with her husband, just as a woman who still longs for recognition from her father will do everything for her partner later on.

Furthermore, the shadow of incest casts a strange inhibition over a couple when they are making love. After all, each of us chooses a love object that can be traced back to our first love. Freud expresses this rather laconically: to find sexual pleasure in a relationship you have to conquer the incest prohibition, otherwise it will not work. He adds that this often works only in a second marriage or a second relationship. It seems as though the first catches all the negative weight of the past.

Sex can be enjoyed only away from the mother.

The link between love and drives is by no means self-evident. As we said earlier, Freud compared their combination to the completion of a tunnel being driven through a hill from both directions. The field of drives that are auto-erotic, partial and solely focused on pleasure is a different field from that of love which is total, reciprocal and

60

focused particularly on the other's desire. When these two fields are so different, the question inevitably arises: how do they ever come together? Experience shows that this does not happen automatically, and that in a number of cases it fails in a very characteristic way.

It is this way that is shown in the film *9½ Weeks*. This is a smooth and aesthetically packaged—and therefore permissible—porn film, a typical commercial remake of the much more powerful and richer original, *Last Tango in Paris*. Two people who do not know each other—with the emphasis on 'not knowing each other'—try out every conceivable sexual variation on each other for nine weeks. Towards the end of the film—the half week—one of the two wants to make the transition to love, the transition from being a partial object to being a person, and starts to reveal a self. As a result, the other person takes flight, and the relationship stops before it starts. The essential precondition, namely the unknown quantity, the lack of subjectivity, no longer existed. This same function can also be seen in the figure of the 'masked man' (or woman), in less cultivated eroticism.

The way in which there is a permanent divide between love and drive is sufficiently problematic for Freud to devote two papers to it: 'A Special Type of Choice of Object made by Men' and 'On the Universal Tendency to Debasement in the Sphere of Love'. Both these works look at the problem from the man's perspective; for a woman, the division will be different. In men, there is the familiar distinction between the Madonna on a pedestal and the lowlife whore, in the sense that they elevate the love object to unknown—and, above all, unattainable—heights. These are the super-conventional husbands who *respect* their wives. They often respect them so much that they become psychologically impotent. The shadow of the forbidden mother covers the beloved in this cloak of respect, so that any sexual approach becomes impossible. However, this impotence wholly melts away, together with the respect, when such a man goes to a whore, either in his imagination or in reality. The pendulum swings the other way, because in this case the woman, in the figure of the whore, is humiliated just as much as the wife-mother is extolled. The dimension of lust appears here, inevitably accompanied by feelings of guilt. It is in this context that we come across the typical male fantasy, well known to every prostitute, of 'saving' a woman. A large number of her clients want to 'save' her from her ruin. They want to restore to her the status of being an object of love. In other words, they want her to become a wife-mother, which brings them back to respect, and completes the circle. Interestingly, in either case, whether he saves her or humiliates her, the power lies with the man. This in itself is a rewrite of the original mother-child scenario. His position has shifted from passive to active.

For a woman, the distinctions are different, though in a sense analogous to those of the man. The same distinction between mother and wife can also be found here, though this time it is not in terms of the love object, but as two different types of identification. If women identify with the mother role, this is at the expense of the other role in which the drive and sexual pleasure are central and vice versa. This is why many a woman becomes sexually active once the children have left—or else when she herself has left or is away from home. The woman, too, has feelings of guilt, but these are experienced mainly in relation to her children, when she feels that she is not adequately fulfilling her role as mother, especially in terms of motherly love. In the opposite case, when she identifies with the role of the wife, the dimension of prohibition and guilt is much less strong, and the importance of the drive and related pleasures increases. In this sense, a woman is much more flexible than a man, whose superego is much stronger in these circumstances. This does not mean that men break the 'rules' less, but it means that their feelings of guilt will be more concerned with the partner than the children. There is a clearer link for men between guilt and pleasure. On the basis of his Oedipal background, where he was subordinate to his father-patriarch, the man experiences prohibitions and the law in a much more absolute way than the woman. The latter has a completely different relationship to this father and the law.

This difference is connected to the fact that within *her* Oedipal background, the woman must change the object of her love, in contrast to the man/son, who can retain his original choice. After all, for a daughter, her mother is also the first and exclusive love object, and she moves towards the father only during a second stage. This move is often only a displacement. The father may be in the foreground, but the figure of the mother (who retains her original importance) is there in the background. This is why lesbian relationships are not directly comparable to male homosexuality. As a result of her early experiences, a woman finds it much easier to adopt a bisexual position. She has already had both sexes as the object of her love, as well as a change of object from one to the other. In contrast, the choice of homosexuality for a man is a much greater step and it is therefore less easily reversible. The fact that, for a girl, the mother was also originally the first object of her love, and this object was exchanged for the father, means that the father was a 'second choice' for her anyway. Consequently, any subsequent partner is at least a 'third choice'. The father as a representative of the law can therefore never have the same weight for a woman as for a man—certainly not when the daughter has in some way got wind of the way in which this representative of the law is sexually dependent on the mother.

One characteristic situation where the link between love and drives fails is when the man remains in the role of the son, and his wife plays the part of the mother. This results in well-known caricatures, particularly the throwback to the traditional Oedipal pattern where the man (son) does his very, very best for his wife (mother), who in this way ends up with another child. Since he wants to be 'everything' for her, he is inexorably condemned to a continual sense of doubt: 'Am I doing it right?' I am using the expression 'Am I doing it right?' deliberately, because this question has a stereotypical effect on erotic behaviour. It is that of a man who always wants to satisfy his wife because only then will he be convinced that he is doing *it* right. However, the criterion he uses is himself and his own male orgasm. He soon starts to put his wife under an *obligation* to climax—which is actually not very conducive to pleasure—particularly as men and women are so different in this respect.

Two sorts of love—Love is giving what you haven't got

It will have become clear by now that, depending on the background, two different types of relationship can develop. The most painful form is the imaginary dual relationship where the forced character can be summarised as follows: *I* insist that *I*, and *I* alone, can fulfil the other person's needs. The opposite applies equally: *I* demand that the other person fulfil *my* needs, and only *mine*. The basic form of this relationship is the Oedipal child who wants to be everything for his/her mother, and to be the only one, as well as demanding the same of her.

This is a mirror love in which the other person must be the same as the self and where no shortcomings are allowed.

The oppressive nature of this sort of relationship becomes manifest in its caricatured form: the boy/girl who tries to do everything for his/her mother later becomes the sort of partner who is always asking, 'What do you think?' 'Is there something wrong?' 'Are you angry?' There is a famous Monty Python sketch *How to Irritate People* that illustrates this brilliantly: the man who takes his girlfriend to a restaurant for the first time and tries to please her so much that she runs away. An excerpt:

- Comfortable?
- Yes, thank you.
- You're not cold, are you?
- No.
- You're not too hot?
- No. I'm fine.
- Sure?
- Yes.
- You would say if you were?
- Yes, I would.
- Promise?
- Yes, I promise.
- And there is no point in saying that you are, just to please me?
- No, honestly, I'm fine.
- Good. You wouldn't prefer to go somewhere else?
- No.
- Quite sure?

- Yes.
- You've only got to give the word and we'll go.
- No really, I like it here.
- Super. Absolutely super. Marvellous. Terrific. You wouldn't prefer to sit over there?
- No.
- Only it's free now. Only, you seem to like that table.
- No. Really.
- Look, would you like to change places with me?
- No.
- Because I don't mind. We'll change places if you want to.
- Not really.
- Look, I'll tell you what. I'll go and take another chair and sit there, and then you can either sit there or where you are now and it won't affect me. OK?
- No.
- Or would you prefer to sit here?
- No.
- You would say?

And so on, until she runs away. In this form, the desire of one person must be exactly the same as the desire of the other. Any difference is a threat and has to be resisted. The demand for exclusive attention will be uncommonly great here. Any third person becomes a potential threat and jealousy is inevitable.

This type of relationship contains a particular assumption, namely that desire and need can actually be completely fulfilled. This assumption appears in a number of forms, from the paranoid certainty that one has 'it', to the constant neurotic doubt ('Am I doing it right?'), the related jealousy ('That person over there has/can do it'), to depression ('I'm nothing, I can't do anything'). The basic attitude remains unchanged, the conviction that one must fulfil the other person's needs and that this is possible in principle.

However, the desire goes back to a structural—and consequently to an irreparable—loss. The division from the Other is final once language has developed between the mother and the child, between the subject and the world. Consequently, within this dual relationship, love will never be wholly satisfying. There is always the hope of even more, even better, with the typical quantitative expression that characterises this imaginary view of the world. The aim of achieving as much sexual gratification as possible in order to express psychological well-being, and therefore health, is undoubtedly one of the greatest myths of modern times—not least, as a result of reading Freud at too simple a level.

The result of this is endless competition, both with regard to 'having', and with regard to 'being'. A man can never 'have' enough to prove his masculinity and in this way fulfil the desires of his partner. This results in the 'Guinness Book of Records' hysteria discussed above. The woman can never 'be' enough of a woman to meet the desires of her partner in this way. This explains the Miss World parades and related masquerades. Men compete with each other with regard to having 'it', and women in being 'it', which leads to different approaches.[7] The culmination of this competition can be found at the point where men compete to be the most beautiful woman, with transvestism, transsexuality, and psychosis as extreme examples of 'gender bending'.

Once again, the underlying assumption is that desire can be wholly fulfilled. Against this myth of perfect reciprocated love, there are two striking statements made by Lacan: 'The man's symptom is his woman' and 'For the woman, the man always means ruin'. These statements can easily be verified in the psychopathology of everyday life. Both are an effect of the imaginary dual relationship. Anyone who closely follows a man for a while will see that he always chooses the same type of woman. This means that after a certain trial period he succeeds in forcing his partners into the same mould, so that they become perfect copies of the previous woman. This explains the second statement: 'For the woman, the man always means ruin'. It is ruin because she is forced into a particular corset, where she is either abused or idolised. In both cases she is destroyed as a separate individual. It is no coincidence that in the wake of the emancipation movement a whole new social class has developed—the educated lonely woman. She is lonely because, unlike her predecessors, she refuses to submit to this ruin.

Today, these two statements might just as well be interchangeable. For a woman, her partner is also a symptom, and for many a man, his wife is a ravager. Thus the group of lonely men is also continuing to grow. This reversal is fairly simple to achieve, because the underlying form of the imaginary dual relationship is not that between a man and a woman, but that between mother and child, quite apart from the specific sex of the child.

The imaginary dual relationship is based on the conviction that it is possible to give/find/get 'it'. In practice, this turns into misery and torture, with the result that there is often a swing to the other extreme, the conviction that nothing is possible, that there is no point in anything, and that everything is the same. This reaction remains within the dual imaginary relationship, though it is now tinged with bitterness and disappointment instead of hope and expectation.

In contrast to this, there is triangular love. The previous form binds two figures within a mirror relationship. Triangular love is based on the idea of a triangle, which inevitably reminds us of the words of La Rochefoucauld: 'the chains of marriage are so heavy to bear that one needs at least two people to carry them, and sometimes three'. These three are the self, the other person, and the lack as such, something that cannot be removed. I heard this formulated best by someone who was coming to the end of his analysis: 'You really have to love someone to leave her alone'—leaving a person alone without immediately paralysing his/her desires and longings with your own contributions and solutions. This allows the other person to actually be different. Eventually, it makes a relationship, based on difference, possible. This is the symbolic triangular form of love based on longing, and therefore it opens up the possibility for creation. The impossibility of fulfilling this longing means that any mirror relationship is a priori doomed to failure, for it is never possible to give what another lacks. However this does not mean that it is not possible to give and to receive.

Triangular love allows for a meeting, a coming together that is possible without being forced. It may happen or it may not. Indeed, you really have to love a person to leave him/her alone. This love starts in the same place as the previous form, in the relationship between the mother and child and the interaction of giving and taking between them. It is a toddler who scribbles a drawing and proudly gives it to his mother, saying 'Sun!'—to which his mother says: 'Oh, what a lovely sun!' It is the father who plays football with his little boy, allows him to win, and tells him he is the best footballer in town. It is my little seven-year-old daughter who discovers the Christmas presents on the

23rd December, hidden behind some rubbish in the cellar, confirming her suspicions all at once, but who still decides to be gladly surprised on Christmas morning. In this tacit relationship, something is received that cannot be given, and one gives something one does not have. To quote Lacan, 'Love means giving what you don't have.'

In all these exchanges there is a dimension of pretence, rather than deceit. Giving something one does not have presupposes that it is possible to get something that is not there. We are aware of this, smile and enjoy it. In this form of love, it is the rule, rather than the exception, to discover two additional aspects: that it is possible to love someone of the same sex without necessarily being homosexual (so much for homophobia!) and that it is possible to love several people at the same time without this entailing a threat to other relationships (so much for jealousy!). These two discoveries have one common feature: the compulsive element of the drive is absent.

Love is poetry

The relationship between sexual partners is certainly not self-evident. At the end of this millennium the biological-genetic aspect is less compulsive than ever before. Love and drives have different requirements and lead to an inner conflict in every person between desire and pleasure. It is this conflict that leads to a need for regulation and protection.

Both of these are dictated by this need. It is always created by the social group, often together with a dictator who is deposed every so often. These dictates can be found in the rules that characterise a culture, particularly the rules which form the structures of relationships, *The Elementary Structures of Kinship*. This classical anthropological study by Lévi-Strauss reveals the fact that these rules can be very different. This, in itself, is proof enough that the one and only *original* relationship between men and women never existed, just as there has never been a one and only original language. These two facts really concern the same thing: structures of relationships are built up on names. This comparison can be extended even further. The explanation for the existence of a certain structure of relationships should not be sought in a better correspondence with the 'natural' aspects of man, just as the arguments for a particular word should not be sought in a better correspondence with the thing it signifies. There is no basic model. Each relational structure takes the place of an original relationship that never existed. So how does a concrete structure of relationships acquire its authority? In exactly the same way as in language—from the group. It is the group convention that determines language and its evolution. This happens quite independently of linguistic 'puritans'. It is the convention of the group that determines relational structures, again quite separately from the other kind of 'puritans'.

Just as a child has to learn the language of the group to which it belongs, a couple must adopt the relationship prescribed by the group. Depending upon the strictness and closed nature of the group, it may or may not be possible to combine this with individual choice. However, just as it is possible to be creative with your mother tongue, you can always make your own contributions. This comparison goes much further: the creation of an individual sexual relationship and the creation of one's own language come together in poetry as the ultimate attempt to express what is missing. This does not mean that every couple should start writing poetry. In fact, there is a much more prosaic approach, literally at the level of prose. Every couple that stays together for a long time develops its own language. They start with a new pet-name—the name chosen for the beloved—and continue with the use of a number of shared expressions that are not comprehensible to the outside world but that, when used, evoke a smile of understanding. A couple's own language, just like any language is based on a convention. In this case it applies only to a group of two. Therefore it is a unique language, creating its own world, including this relationship. The language created in this way evokes a reality beyond the word and is truly original. A typical characteristic of this is humour as the royal road to what can only be evoked, but never put into words. This is undoubtedly one of the differences between being in love and love. People who are in love take themselves seriously, so that there is never room for humour. Despite all the lightness and butterflies in the stomach associated with it, being in love is a rather heavy condition and leaves little space for anything else. On the other hand, humour creates space where it evokes something beyond what it says, and therefore allows space for the other person.

Just as a child has to learn the language of the group to which it belongs, a couple must adopt the relationship prescribed by the group. Depending upon the strictness and closed nature of the group, and depending upon the extent to which people can themselves cope with freedom, they will or will not be able to make their own contribution to this relationship. This means that we are confronted here with another issue—the question of authority.

II. Fathers in Flight

*'The general, supra-temporal, strict superego is an
out-of-date analytical fiction.'*
(Sloterdijk 1997)

*'Is it true that one must dive to the depths of the sea and
save one's father to become a real boy?'*
(Auster 1982)

In recent years, a lot of attention has been paid to the subject of bullying at school. A large-scale scientific research project on this subject conducted by several researchers over several months came to the following statistically supported, and therefore scientifically bona fide results: one, there is more bullying at school than at home; two, there is more bullying during breaks than during classes; three, children with a physical defect—obesity (fatty!), astigmatism (cross-eyes!)—are bullied more than others. Sometimes science is all too simple. This reminds me of an unforgettable quotation from the discussion in the *Times Literary Supplement* about *The Encyclopaedia of Banality*: 'Moose are frequently found in large numbers in many parts of Canada.'

So what about bullying? Sometimes human sciences are an attempt to formulate things that have already been said more succinctly elsewhere. In her splendid autobiography, Doris Lessing makes the following remark in passing: 'Children have always been bullies and will always continue to be bullies. The question is not so much what is wrong with our children; the question is why adults and teachers nowadays cannot handle it anymore'. Not being able to cope has now taken all sorts of excessive forms, and

73

references are even made to bullied parents and bullied teachers at every level of the educational system.

This is extrapolated in child psychiatry. Those working in that field complain that they see fewer psychiatric symptoms but are increasingly confronted with problems related to upbringing. Therefore child psychiatry is reduced to a process of re-education that always fails. The reason for the failure lies in the question we saw above in Doris Lessing's remark: there is something wrong with authority. The function of authority, which used to be a self-evident truth embodied in many different figures, has now disappeared. The fact that the basis for bringing up children disappeared at the same time can be seen in everyday life. Optimists maintain that teachers and parents now have to make sure that they 'deserve' their authority—they have to earn it. However, experience has shown that the authority that remains usually consists of pure power, and, further, such power exists only if it is visible and tangible.[1]

In other words: where have all the fathers gone? In this respect, our century has made a 180-degree turn, almost unnoticed. In the first half of the century, there was the bearded, moustachioed, monocled patriarch, full of a sense of his own importance, lord and master at least in his own home and preferably as far as possible outside it. His authority was hardly a matter of personal merit. He merely assumed it automatically, and it was questioned by only a few. At the beginning of the second half of this century, the balance started to tip the other way, and since the 1960s, any form of authority has become automatically suspect. Freud and Marx became the intellectual fathers in whose name fathers were banished, as a source of frustration and therefore neurosis to one, and a source of exploitation and abuse to the other. Students in T-shirts and jeans campaigned against the uniformity of the army and industry. Education took place in freedom and an anti-authoritarian approach was a must. The feminist movement made its own contribution and there was a wave of social change which unwittingly swept aside its own foundations. In sociological terms, this was described as the evolution from an authoritarian system to a system based on negotiation, 'the medium is the message'. The aim was freedom for everyone, and in particular for those who were oppressed in the past—the woman and the child.

From the beginning the links with feminism were clear, and in several respects this was essential. The woman was the most oppressed figure in the patriarchal system. Even the lowest man in the pecking order could still get rid of his frustrations at home. As John Lennon sang: 'Woman is the nigger of the world'. In 1970, Germaine Greer published her famous book, *The Female Eunuch*, undoubtedly an intellectual milestone in the second feminist wave. Like this second wave, the scope of this book extends beyond feminist issues. It is aimed at Liberation with a capital 'L' and is directed against the structure of the state, against the traditional family, and against authority. Germaine Greer formulated this very succinctly in the final sentence of her first chapter: 'The opponents of female suffrage lamented that woman's emancipation would mean the end of marriage, morality and the state. When we reap the harvest which the unwitting suffragettes sowed we shall see that the anti-feminists were after all right.'

Meanwhile, twenty-five years later, we can reap the harvest and see that Greer's prophetic words have become true in many respects. Surprisingly enough, she does not seem to be satisfied with her own predictions at all—on the contrary. In an interview with the *Sunday Times*

Magazine (UK, March 3, 1996) she submitted that if women were to come into power, Great Britain would decline in a very short time to the level of a developing country, with no power or influence. The rest of the interview was along the same lines.

This sort of volte-face is quite incomprehensible, and makes us look for something with which to sweep it aside in some cosy rationalisation—she's probably frustrated, it's her age, her hormones. Indeed, her most recent publication, *The Whole Woman*, implies a return to a black and white opposition between male-oppressor and woman-victim. The strange thing is that we find a comparable development in another figurehead of the same movement, Doris Lessing, though formulated rather more subtly. Anyone who has read her four-novel sequence, *Children of Violence* , would not for a second doubt her leftist feminist commitment, nor her literary talent. Yet in her recent autobiography and in the interviews about it, she distances herself from both from this form of feminism and from her erstwhile Marxism and regrets the impact it had on her personal life.

In the meantime, Camille Paglia had become an immediate cult figure with her *Sexual Personae*. Hers is a daring position—as a woman and committed lesbian, she presents a fiery plea for the male principle and criticises femininity in a way which no man has dared to do since Otto Weininger's *Sex and Character*.[2] These outbursts are not isolated events—far from it. They surprise only because of their source. However, the ideas contained in them are almost universal at the end of this century. The call for law and order is fairly widespread, from the populist desire for brute fascism to the dream of many intellectuals of an enlightened dictatorship. Both forget the experiences of history. An ironic change can be found in the field of psychotherapy, where attempts are made on all sides to introduce what was abolished twenty years ago ('More structure!'). The psychopathology resulting from the excesses of those days is reflected in reverse in the problems we have now.

Seen in these terms, it seems to be a matter of balance— authority is necessary, but not too much, and parents have to be re-educated to restore this balance in relation to their children. It seems that no one is able to provide such re-education, so that both parents and children continue to be faced with a shortcoming. They are united together aboard a sinking ship whose captain was thrown overboard during an earlier mutiny. Where are the fathers of yesteryear?

Freud, the Oedipus of his time

The father of psychoanalysis is surely the man who elevated the importance of the father to previously unknown heights. In itself, this was nothing new, and it had happened before, though from a religious angle. What was new was, ironically, that it was a free-thinking Jew who imbued the traditional religious position with a *scientific* character. In fact, this comparison can be extended even further. Those of his followers, who later focused on the position of the mother, were inevitably banished from the orthodox analytical church. Mothers and women were superfluous.

It is worth taking a closer look at the position Freud assigns to the father. Re-reading his case studies and their accompanying theoretical conceptualisations reveals a curious gap between theory and practice. In virtually all of the cases, the father of his patient turns out to be a weak figure, the opposite of someone who radiates authority and strength. At best, he was simply an invalid who required long-term care, usually from the person who later became the patient. Otherwise, he was a failure. One lived off the fortune of his wife, whom he had chosen for this reason. Another wandered from one spa town to another, a melancholy figure. A third used his daughter as a device to divert his mistress's husband—a mistress who was not much use to him anyway, because he was impotent.[3]

The reader therefore expects that this will be reflected in some way in the theory, a conclusion along the lines: weak fathers, neurotic children. It is a big surprise when he comes across the opposite conclusion every time: the Freudian father is depicted as a feared and threatening figure who instils enormous fear in his children. At this point, the children are sons because the daughters do not yet count. The reason Freud gives for this fear is as simple as it is astonishing—the child desires to possess his mother sexually, but finds his father in his way, a father who furiously chases him from the bedroom. This is meant to explain the typical form that this fear takes—a fear of castration. The rest of the theory follows automatically. Because of this fear, the little boy becomes good and obedient, that is, he identifies with his father. The result of this is the psychoanalytic construction of the conscience, the development of the superego. Little Johnny grows into big John, who later repeats the same process with John junior.

The contrast between this element of Freud's theory and the detailed descriptions of his case studies is so great that in some instances it cannot be ignored. The most extreme example is in the only study where the subject is a male child, Hans. Instead of the expected interpretation of the theory, we find exactly the opposite. The threats of castration are on the part of the mother. The father is dominated by her in the presence of the son, whose love is above all for his father. When we then read that the little boy's hysteria and fear must be related to his fear of this man, it is clear that something is not right. Either Freud is completely blind, or the theory must be thoroughly revised. This revision is the subject of a later case study, but once again it is rather surprising. While everyday reality is different from the situation considered to be normal by Freud—a frightening father who threatens castration, the son in love with his mother, who is completely passive—the child will always call upon a reality of another order. According to Freud, there is a reality that is stored in the collective unconscious of the human race. This hyperreality is said to dominate the 'real' reality, and in this way it determines the psychology of the individual.

This hyperreality has gone down in history as Freud's myth about the primal horde, and it is here that the status of the Freudian father is confirmed. In fact, the idea of myth and hyperreality does not mean that, in Freud's mind, it is only a story. On the contrary, he believes that this once really happened, probably between the last Ice Ages. The significance he attaches to the myth is very far-reaching. He recognises in it the basis of the social order as such. Before this time, there was a herd of animals; after it, an organised horde of people. The fact that a number of Freud's biographers saw this, above all, as the basis of the psychoanalytic hordes, is best left out of consideration here.

For anyone who does not know the story, Freud's *Totem and Taboo* is about a primeval father—a sort of silverback, as in the mountain gorillas—who dominates all the females and keeps all the young males, that is, his sons, fearful and at a distance. At a certain point, these sexually frustrated males unite in a brotherhood and kill their greatly feared father with the aim of gaining sexual access to the females. According to the myth, the murder is followed by an acute sense of guilt that forms the foundation both for the prohibition on killing and for the prohibition on incest. Thus the murdered primal father is the foundation for the social system and the brotherhood becomes the first social unit. According to Freud's argument, the memory of the primal father and the primal murder has in some way been stored in the collective memory, resulting in a universal sense of guilt and the prohibition on incest, which forms the foundation for any form of human society. In this sense, the myth has the same role as the creation myth.

Today, even to a seasoned Freudian, this story is not really convincing. It does not contain a mother figure, and the females do not have a separate status. At the very least, the sudden appearance of a sense of guilt after the murder is rather surprising. The way in which the tale is stored in the collective memory is not at all clear, just as the way in which Freud's patients bypass the opposite reality is also unclear. Nor does the fact that the foundation of human culture was attributed, almost arbitrarily, exclusively to males make it any more acceptable.

This version of the story is the best known. Another version that appeared fairly late in Freud's career and that was developed in quite a different context, in his study *Moses and Monotheism* , is much less well known. The first version concerned only the father's power over his sons. The second version delineates the relationship between patriarchy and matriarchy, with the son in between.

This time, the story has several stages. In the first place, there is the primal father and his females—there are no references to mothers, and language as such has not yet developed. The murder of the primal father takes place at a second stage and quite unexpectedly. This gives rise to the establishment of a matriarchy—the mothers take power. The third stage was a big headache for Freud. He saw this as a transitional stage characterised by a curious mixture of matriarchy, mother-goddesses, clans of brothers and the start of totemism. The fourth and last stage sees the reintroduction of the primal father/patriarch, now elevated to divine heights, and this reintroduction is performed by the sons, often by the youngest among them.

It is this same process—above all, the last stage—that Freud recognises in the development of the major monotheistic religions, where Judaism sets the tone, with Christianity and Islam as later local variations. The 'sons' —Moses, Jesus and Mohammed—each revealed God the Father in their own way. Moses installed Yahweh against the preceding pluralism of gods, Jesus confirmed the status of a divine father separate from the woman-mother, and Mohammed completed the line with Allah. Freud ignored the fact that primal murder is much less obvious in these religions and their related stories, which, moreover, concern the son rather than the father. From the time that this myth was established through the son, every actual father acquired power through the collective belief in a primal father/god.

A further analysis of this second version of the myth reveals a number of striking new points. It is the son who (re)installs the father, and does so in the face of a female power that is experienced as a threat. It seems that there is not so much a fear of the father but a *need* for this father figure in order to keep another danger at bay. This danger becomes fully visible only when the father has disappeared, and this threat is related to femaleness.

In other words, the father is the symptom of the son.

Oedipus on the wrong track

Whether Freud's story contains a factual truth—as he himself was convinced it did—is irrelevant to us. Lévi-Strauss showed us that a myth is always an attempt to cast an underlying structure in an epic form. Thus it becomes a collective story that serves as a framework for a previous psychological reality and, at the same time, determines the subsequent one. In the example above, this is indeed the case. The invented myth is merely one version of something that can be found in different forms in historical anthropology. Actually, Freud's version of the story is rather poor compared to other versions. There are certainly many stories describing the power relationship between mother-goddesses and the patriarchal system. The most important tragedy in this context is not *Oedipus Rex* (Sophocles) but *The Oresteia* (Aeschylus).

I shall return later to this presumed development, with the intention of making a distinction between the story told retrospectively and the need for this in contrast with what is known in history. What I want to focus on for the moment is the close link between authority, in the sense of patriarchal authority, and the determination of psychosexual identity in the sense of, how should one be a man, how should one be a woman. There is a trendy term for this—gender identity.

The establishment of patriarchy always comes down to the installation of the One Man. It makes little difference whether he is the primal father or God the Father. From that moment, the power factor is linked to one sex that immediately designates the other sex as inferior. It is no coincidence that the daily male prayer of the most traditional monotheistic patriarchal religion—Judaism—contains the following line: 'Blessed art Thou, O Lord our God, King of the Universe, that Thou has not made me a woman'. In the wake of this, there is a very strong differentiation between the two sexes. Thus, with little exaggeration, it may be said that the current distinction between man and woman regarding gender identity is the result of a monotheistic patriarchal system. This distinction always leads to an inferior position for women. These religions profess as much publicly, and it is installed by the patriarchal system. Another result that concerns us less here but that is very important historically, is the need for conversion. Every system which believes it has access to the one and only truth considers others outside the system to be inferior, fodder for conversion and colonisation.

The familiar effect of this is that male identity is always described in positive terms—and conversely, female identity in negative terms—with the best known oppositions being strong for men and weak for women, intelligent versus stupid, brave versus fearful. At the same time, most monotheistic patriarchal cultures created a situation that established and reinforced these characteristics. The resultant effect—male superiority, female inferiority—endorsed the original argument and operated as a self-fulfilling prophecy.

The question now is what happens when such a patriarchy starts to topple. This necessarily has an effect on gender identity and the related prescribed role patterns. The fact that this patriarchal monotheistic complex is foundering at the end of the millennium is quite clear and it is happening in a very distinctive way. The difference from previous periods of instability in history is that in the past, the underlying principle was never or hardly ever questioned. At most, there was a replacement in which one primal father was substituted for another ('The King is dead, long live the King!'), Moses by Christ, Christ by Mohammed, both by Marx, and so forth. The belief in the unique system as such was retained and in all cases there was virtually no difference from the previous system as regards the male-female relationship. On the other hand, the principle itself is tottering in the second half of the twentieth century. The ancient gods are being removed from their pedestals, together with the stories about them, and there is no convincing replacement available. This means that nowadays we can virtually read Freud's myth the other way round, so that a sort of collective regression can be seen, a return to what preceded the monotheistic patriarchal complex.

First of all, the myth in the reverse form means that the son can no longer see his father as a representative of the past and as someone who hands down paternal authority. As a result, the father no longer provides a sense of security against an underlying danger and the sons become more and more fearful and search for an alternative. Among other ways, the extent of this fear can be found in the aggression that follows from it, since aggression is one of the most characteristic ways of expressing fear. The danger that had been concealed now emerges, once the protection from it disappears. For a while, its nature remains unclear. The only clue that Freud's myth offers is that it is related to femininity.

The disappearance of the father-patriarch means that the sons have lost their central role model for identification. The result is that they are condemned to remain in the position of the son, in the absence of a model that would enable them to make the transfer to an adult position. Thirty-year-old teenagers and forty-year-old adolescents are by no means exceptional these days, and form a new psychiatric category that has been in the headlines for the last ten years. The so-called borderline patient is best described as an adult operating at the pre-Oedipal level, the level that precedes that of the impact of the paternal function.

Not every son stays a son, but what happens to him if his father is missing as a model to identify with? In the absence of such a model, a number of sons look in the other direction and consequently become perfect mothers. The developments in this field can be clearly seen in the world of film. *Kramer v. Kramer* (1979) is the story of a typical immature husband abandoned by his wife ('It used to be the other way round, you know'). Since he loves his son, he does his best, and by the end of the film he has actually become the perfect mother who can therefore go on looking after his child. Fifteen years later, exactly the same story is repeated in *Mrs Doubtfire* (1993), although the solution is extended even further this time. Robin Williams actually has to metamorphose into a woman-mother in order to become an 'adult'. Meanwhile, Dustin Hoffman underwent the same metamorphosis in *Tootsie* (1992), this time simply to make a living, something that Dame Edna had already been doing for a number of years.

The message is clear, and the irony of history lies in this reversal. While a woman had to copy a man in the past to 'get there', things are now moving in exactly the opposite direction. This actually provides a new interpretation for the double morality of the past—of course men should allow their feminine characteristics to come out, and of course women should have equal opportunities in employment. However, in the business world—where the real power lies—the traditional climate prevails and in order to succeed, women have to behave like men.

For daughters, a different process applies: the disappearance of the automatic superiority of the male also implies the disappearance of female inferiority, a fact that was once accepted without question. Currently the majority of West European universities have more female than male students, and this trend is continuing. As a result, daughters are escaping from the restrictions of the past and are entering the world looking for an equal partner. The commercial expression of this can be found in soft porn videos when a woman goes on top of her partner and actively rides him. Confronted with this demand, many of the sons we have just looked at take flight, because there is no safety there, and they are terrified. The effect of this is that more and more young women are going into relationships with a much older partner whom they see as a man who has come to terms with this underlying fear and who can therefore approach a woman as an equal. This is in contrast to the eternal adolescent who opts for the safety of the group and for whom sex works only if he is the boss.

This adolescent becomes extremely predictable for a woman. The majority have seen through this man after a few years of experience and know exactly how to behave to elicit a particular response. If they act slightly vulnerable, the man immediately becomes a Saviour, smiling broadly. A soupçon of assertive feminism combined with an element of independence, and the man becomes a Hunter. A generous laugh and the right clothes, direct eye contact—but leaving the initiative to him—and he becomes the Seducer. An evening of wild sex and the moody moaner turns into the sweetie he used to be. The only thing that is not possible is independence, a position separate from his. Is it surprising that many women 'give up' on men after a while and start looking for a girlfriend? Going back to the origin of the myth, we therefore come to the actual primal father. The loss of his self-evident authority has the result that the sons group together and start looking for a real authority. The effect of this is that all sorts of primary primal fathers emerge, each with their own primal horde, seemingly offering a safe haven. These sons are facing a big disappointment, because it soon becomes clear that such real primal fathers are ultimately out for only one thing, as is every primal father—their own pleasure.

What about mothers? They are an abandoned category, increasingly sentenced to live alone with their children, among whom they often include their partner of the moment. They have most trouble with their sons, while there seems to be a new coalition developing with their daughters.

The net result of all this is the lonely emancipated woman, thirty-year-old adolescents in groups, lonely divorced men who stay alone because of their fear, and one-parent families. The human condition in a new guise.

The traditional solution

The belief in the collective stories that form the foundation of the monotheistic patriarchal culture has disappeared, and there does not seem to be an immediate replacement. The resulting shifts in these role patterns give rise to fear and confusion, leading to the predictable call for law and order. In fact, the traditional solution is always an attempt to return to the old order, and there are even signs of fundamentalism. This could already be seen in Freud himself. When he was confronted with the neurotic fears of a five-year-old boy in the case mentioned above, he did everything he could to restore the boy's father to the position he believed he should have.

From a historical perspective, this is extremely ironic because, in social terms, this solution inevitably leads to a phallocratic fascism and the last version of this almost succeeded in exterminating Freud's own people. It reminds me of a famous scene from Bob Fosse's film, *Cabaret*, in which the depiction of decadence and dissolution comes to an end when a fair-haired—and therefore racially pure—young man in his Hitler Youth uniform stands up to sing an equally pure song, thus announcing the start of a new order. This film is actually about an impotent, frightened young man who is put to rights by a strong-minded young woman. The imaginary primal fathers of fascism are no more than attempts to rein in the danger in women. It is no coincidence that the great masters of totalitarian regimes could tolerate only young girls whom they could patronise, or child women as sexual partners. The biographies of Hitler and Mao leave us in no doubt in this respect, and similar phenomena are reflected nowadays in the ever-increasing occurrence of paedophilia. This serves as a measure of the increasing fear that men have of confronting women as independent sexual partners, with their own desires and pleasures.

The effect of the traditional solution is, among other things, a clear division of roles between the sexes—the son-warrior, the pure virgin, the childbearing mother and the omnipresent, primal father. This was described and studied at length by Klaus Theweleit in his two-volumed *Male Fantasies*, now a famous work. The book studies the emergence of fascism on the basis of 'subsidiary materials': the posters from the time, the caricatures, the novels, the pamphlets and the like. In these, the division of roles becomes increasingly clear, as well as the underlying fear of women. Men are presented as defenders of law and order, glowing with health and fighting for their country. Women are purity itself, fair-haired, virginal, passively waiting for the one role that is their goal in life—to bear new sons. However, their dangerous alter-ego can be seen in the background, the woman as a greedy vamp, as a centre of decadent pleasure where the man is constantly in danger of being sucked in and against which he must defend himself with an increasingly strong brotherhood with other men. The fact that Klaus Theweleit wrote the book to come to terms with his fascist father and the associated history makes this book a psychoanalytic therapy that goes further than Freud himself. Ultimately Freud could not get beyond the father, nor—therefore—the traditional solution.

In so far as any justification is given for this traditional solution—in particular, the attempts at reintroducing a primal father and the related fundamentalism—references are usually made to the progress believed to be inherent in the monotheistic patriarchal complex. For example, Freud's description of monotheism shows that he considered it superior in every way to the previous belief in many gods. The same train of thought can be found in certain anthropological studies, where the emergence of a patriarchy at a later date is seen as cultural progress, in comparison with what is presumed to be a preceding matriarchy. In fact, these two phenomena—monotheism and patriarchy—are two sides of the same coin.

For a long time this position was considered self-evident on the basis of the conviction that history always moves in a progressive direction, ever faster, higher and better. This naïve idea of progress has now, just as obviously, been rejected. In fact, the same thing applies to the opposite idea, namely that it was so much better in the past, in the good old days. This illusion is at least as persistent as the idea of progress, and quintessentially both views reveal a sense of discontent with the here and now.

Whatever the case may be, the idea that monotheism entails progress, is no longer quite so obvious. Karen Armstrong wrote a fascinating study in which she went in search of the history of God, in a style combining the historical studies of Barbara Tuchmann and the British thrillers of P. D. James—i.e., three women. One of the surprising conclusions to emerge from her work is that monotheistic religions, certainly when combined with a patriarchal incarnation, are always among the cruellest and least tolerant in the history of the human race. A conviction that one is always right in matters where there is absolutely no proof, combined with this incarnation, reduces the non-believer to an inferior being who has only two alternatives—to convert or to die. 'Kill them all, God will sort them out'.

Therefore it is not surprising that in the context of feminism and the breakdown of patriarchy, there was a move towards a different kind of society, a more loving, milder and more humane one—in other words, a more feminine society. The combination of an ecological back to (mother) nature movement and a misunderstood chapter in historical anthropology gave rise to yet another myth, that of the matriarchal society. At first sight, this does not seem to differ very much from any other '-archy'; it is simply one in which women have the power, although there is a presumption that they will exercise this power much more peacefully. However, there is little or no change in the power structure as such.

Actually the question is whether this society would really be so peace loving. According to Elias Canetti, power is always postponed violence, and I see no reason why women should be an exception to this, certainly when there is an assumption that the power structure as such remains unchanged. In any case, this solution is based on a completely erroneous understanding of history. The matriarchal society, which is often presented in rather hazy, romantic, pastel colours, has never existed. Ethnological studies of people in our own century who are still living in the stone age, as well as historical and anthropological research, make it possible to reconstruct original primitive societies. Again and again, these reveal that this history is much more complex than a simple reversal. Nevertheless, these studies certainly provide us with some clues to explain our current patterns of relationships.

'Filling your belly comes first, ethics come later!'

Consequently we must look to history, in combination with ethnology and anthropology. One of the effects of emancipation and feminism is that many female researchers studied these subjects in the hope of discovering an original matriarchal Atlantis. One of these women was Evelyn Reed, an American socialist feminist who worked for twenty years on her magnum opus, *Woman's Evolution*, and found to her surprise that her results were quite different from what she had expected.

In this sort of research project the following two questions are nearly always raised: what are the rules that characterise a particular people, and what sort of society do

91

they live in? Such studies inevitably reflect the researcher's own society and the researcher unconsciously uses him/herself as a measure of comparison. Therefore these issues actually come down to the following questions. What are a society's rules with regard to sexuality, and what is their version of the family? After all, for us sex is subject to the most rules, particularly within our family structure.

Therefore it was a great surprise to find that this does not apply elsewhere. In fact, researchers did not even realise it at first. Hordes of early missionaries and ethnologists wrote descriptions on the 'family' in a particular tribe and were always astonished or irritated by their extremely promiscuous behaviour, often combined with an (apparent) lack of knowledge about biological paternity. It was only much later in (post) modern anthropology that the radically different nature of societies was appreciated.

These radical differences are based in the first place on a different set of values. In primitive people the first—and yet, most important—object to be regulated is not sexuality, but *food*. All the important original rules—known as taboos—concern this and, for example, determine in great detail who can eat what, when, with whom, and in what way. The segregation based on these taboos relating to food is so extensive that it ultimately determines the social organisation of the tribe in great detail. Where groups form, the same divisions are found again and again—on the one hand, mothers and children, and on the other hand, the hunters united together in one clan, but separated by strict rules on food.

We can only uess at the reason for this original taboo; presumably, it i› related to the scarcity of food and to the related phenomenon of cannibalism. Examinations of archaeological kitchen waste show that *Homo homini lupus* really did exist, and anyone who is constantly preoccupied with survival has little time left for sex.

It is almost impossible to discover whether cannibalism was once an historically universal phenomenon. However, beyond this factual reality, we can presume an imaginary reality that goes beyond the mere need for food. Anthropological studies of cannibalism reveal reasons for this phenomenon other than hunger. The natives of New Guinea eat their enemy not because they are hungry, but in order to assimilate his 'soul'. In this light, the original fear of the mother/woman takes a very concrete form. It is the fear of disappearing back into that first other person. The observable fact that one first emerged from the body of that other person means that it can be quite conceivable to return to it. Is it a coincidence that being devoured is a constantly recurring, frightening theme in many fairy tales, or that many mythical cosmologies have stories about either devouring someone or being devoured? In classical Greek tragedy it is the female Sphinx who devours people, and it was Oedipus who was the first to escape. Another well-known anthropological phenomenon can be seen in the same line of argument. The original taboos on food always prohibit eating anything from one's own totem animal, that which is part of the most intimate aspect of one's own group and also gives the group its name. This is permitted only as a great exception and on certain solemn occasions. I will return to this early form of Holy Communion later. The taboos on food can be traced back to an original prohibition—the prohibition on becoming reincorporated or 're-embodied'.

The first social organisation or 'clan' developed on the basis of these food taboos. In its primary form, a clan comprises two subgroups. The first subgroup consists of the women and children, with the proviso that the male children must make the transition to the second subgroup, the subgroup of men, at a particular age. This transition, which normally occurs at puberty, is always accompanied by initiation rituals, giving the man a new status, and above all, subjecting him to many new rules. From this time onward, the adult son can no longer eat with the women and smaller children, and inter-relationships are strictly regulated with particular attention paid to separation and purification rituals whenever blood is involved—hunting and war, menstruation and birth. This second subgroup in the clan is also separated in space and assigned its own place: the 'men's hut'. Within one and the same clan, sexual intercourse between the members of these two subgroups is not permitted, and sexual partners must come from another clan.

In turn, every clan is a part of a group of clans, and there are many more taboos and rules among these, mainly concerned with eating and being eaten. For example, there is a clear distinction between what is 'impure' in terms of food for one clan, which may not apply for another clan, and vice versa, so that there can be exchange. Sexual relations are possible between the adult female members of one clan and the adult male members of another clan.

This kind of social structure is described as a *matrilineal* structure, because the binding relationships apply only on the side of the women/mothers. In fact, every clan consists of two maternal subgroups: women, that is mothers, their adult daughters and small children on the one hand, and men, that is sons of these mothers, on the other hand. They are all each other's half-brothers and the half-brothers of their adult sisters in the female group. Therefore, within the clan, everyone is related in a family but exclusively on the mother's side. The father—or rather, the sexual partner—belongs to a completely different clan and does not form part of the most intimate circle.

This has certain very far-reaching effects, and the last traces of these can still be found today, in particular the fact that the sense of loyalty originally applied exclusively along the matrilineal side, that is, via the mother. In clans this is reflected in the production and distribution of food, and everything is always sent to one's own clan as far as possible. This loyalty does not exist towards the sexual partner who belongs to another clan.

For us, the most striking aspect is that there seem to be no fathers, and that sex has barely come into the picture up to now. How does this work? There is a taboo on sexual intercourse within the clan. The subgroups of women/daughters and sons/brothers are forbidden to each other, which immediately suggests the idea of a sort of original prohibition on incest. However, this ban is quite different from the kind we know and expect, because, by its very nature, such a taboo has nothing to do with an Oedipal prohibition relating to the father. There are no fathers. The prohibition on sexual intercourse within the clan is a result of the food taboos and the resulting segregation between the two subgroups of a given clan arising from this. Sexual intercourse is permitted between different clans and is then subject to few or no restrictions—at least, in comparison with the food taboos and viewed from the perspective of western European Victorian morality. That is why there were so many stories about the sexual promiscuity of primitive people during the colonial era.

This undoubtedly had an effect on the attraction of the colonies. The famous 'missionary' position is the term used by the women of New Caledonia to describe the stereotyped sex of the white man. Promiscuity in this context meant, above all, that there was no question of a long-term relationship as a couple, or of any loyalty to one sexual partner. It was this phenomenon, above all, that gave rise to indignation in western Europeans. Not only did these savages engage in premarital sex, there wasn't even any marriage.

It is clear that these forms of society have a fundamentally different structure from our own. Not only are there no fathers, there are no mothers either, but a collective of women with a collective of brothers in the same clan. In fact the terms, 'mother', 'father', and 'brother' do not apply, because these are the names for *our own* family structure. Despite all our attempts to apply these labels, they simply do not exist.

This fundamental difference is also expressed in something that we find inconceivable, namely, that in this sort of society the individual does not exist. The word 'I' is almost absent from primitive languages and stories. The name of the clan is always substituted. The individual *is* the clan and there is a complete fusion between the individual and the group. There is nothing outside the groups except other groups. Within each individual group, there is barely any hierarchy because this would require a sense of self, nor is there any question of individual possessions. This is why references are often made to so-called primitive communism. The loyalty is strictly clan-bound and therefore matrilineal. There are no bonds with the sexual partner, because he belongs to a different clan.

This social structure is far removed from the imagined matriarchy, with some sort of queen at the top of the ladder. The organisation of matrilineal clans is based upon an essentially different structure, of which only the last vestiges remain in our own patriarchal system: ritual greetings with food, pure and impure food, periods of fasting, atonement rituals, vestiges that no longer have anything to do with their origin precisely because they are in a completely new structure. Therefore the next question is—how did this change come about?

In anthropology, this is described as the evolution of matrilineal clan systems towards the so-called *matrifamily*, which is, in turn, a transitional stage towards patriarchy. The matrifamily is the earlier matrilineal clan with one big difference: the male sexual partner who comes from another clan stays to eat with the clan of the woman. The man moves in and there is a couple, not because they sleep together, but because they *eat* together and therefore flout the original extremely strict food taboos. At the same time, this means that in the matrifamily the individual emerges for the first time.

This results in a conflict of loyalties in the matrifamily. All loyalties are clan-related, but the two sexual partners who eat together belong to different clans. In the old system, the woman's loyalty was exclusively to her own clan, that is, to the group of women and children, together with the related group of brothers and sons. Similarly, the loyalty of her male sexual partners was to their own clan, another group of mothers and children and the related group of brothers and sons. It should be noted that in this system the man is obligated through a sense of loyalty to children who could never be his own biological children. The first anthropologists interpreted this as the 'uncle', the mother's brother, taking on fatherhood as a role, in what was then described as an 'avuncular' system. This word was always used in the plural sense to include all the mothers' brothers (who were in fact the only adult males belonging to the clan).

The creation of the matrifamily, where the sexual partners also share food, cuts across the loyalties of the earlier system. Breaking through the clan structure inevitably leads to a conflict of loyalties, particularly when the notion of possession developed. To whom does a man owe his loyalty? To the clan of the sexual partner whose food he is now eating, or to the original clan? What happens to the food and the possessions that are acquired? This conflict crystallises when the first son is born. There is an obvious reason for this. A daughter would stay in the mother's clan anyway, in her own subgroup of women/daughters. However, the son should be sent to the subgroup of the men/sons when he is initiated as an adult, but the question is—to which one? To the subgroup in the mother's original clan, as was the case in the past, or to the subgroup that is part of the original clan of the father?

In this way the firstborn sons became a bone of contention between the two systems. This reveals the reasons for a custom that has survived since time immemorial: the sacrifice of this bone of contention, the firstborn son, usually in a diluted form of the sacrifice of a firstborn male animal. A price must be paid for the recognition of the heir, and it is with this price that fatherhood as such is acknowledged. In this version of the ancient myth of the primal horde, this means that it is the *son* who is killed so that the Kingdom of the Father can be established—a familiar story.

In the course of evolution this sacrifice gradually assumed a more prosaic character. Historically, it led to the first form of a dowry, the sum which a man pays for the children produced from his union with a woman. He pays the sum to the woman's clan, the group that must surrender these children. That is why the dowry must be repaid when the union remains childless. It is a condition of this evolution that a number of other features have developed at the same time: possession, and as a result, a hierarchy and the power that accompanies it. Above all, in the background, there is an awareness of being an individual, a single person, though torn by different desires and loyalties from the very beginning.

Traditional tales and historical reality

According to Evelyn Reed, this transition from the matrilineal to the patriarchal society is such an enormous change that the effects are reflected in a number of traditional tales that try to express an intangible historical reality in epic form. In this sense, she adopts the same view as Lévi-Strauss did in his study of myths. She successfully reinterprets a number of Greek tragedies, assuming that the conflicts of loyalty in these stories must be the central theme and therefore provide a key to their structure as a whole. The two great plays to which I will refer from her study are *Oedipus Rex* by Sophocles and *The Oresteia* by Aeschylus, because each deals with this problem of loyalty in its own particular way.

The first surprise is the fact that the central theme in the classical tragedy of Oedipus is not the incest between mother and son, but the murder of the father, that is the ultimate crime in a patriarchal society. The story is familiar, but it has a different emphasis. Oedipus is a firstborn son and therefore falls between two loyalties, loyalty to the mother's clan and loyalty to the father's clan, and it is predicted that he will kill the father. He is not sacrificed but is

99

abandoned as an orphan, with holes bored through his feet, and left to die. By chance he is saved and grows up with the king and queen of Corinth, convinced that they are his parents. He consults the oracle at Delphi and learns that he will kill his father and marry his mother. Horrified, he flees to Thebes, but on the way he meets a man at a crossroads, quarrels with him and kills him. The tragedy lies in the fact that he has unwittingly murdered his real father, while he was actually fleeing to avoid this. He continues on his way and arrives in the city, where he solves the riddle of the Sphinx, thus escaping from her clutches. Out of gratitude, the people of Thebes ask him to be their king, and so he marries the widowed queen, his own mother. Subsequently the city is destroyed by a punishment sent by the gods. According to the oracle of Delphi, this is because the murder of Laius (the former king who had been found murdered by the roadside) has remained unpunished. Oedipus goes in search of the murderer and discovers the truth—he has killed his own father. Jocasta, his mother/wife, commits suicide, and he puts out his own eyes and goes into exile.

It should be noted that the curse on the city and the punishment of the protagonists is wholly related to the patricide and that Apollo demands through the oracle that the patricide be punished. The particular stress placed on the incest dates from post-Freudian interpretations.

Who is Oedipus? He is the son at the cross-roads of two clans, and, above all, between two systems. He has to choose. It is no coincidence that the commandment of Delphi is 'Know thyself'. Who are you, where do you belong? Is he the son of his mother, who therefore belongs in her clan with the subgroup of sons/brothers and consequently shares her power, or is he the son of his father and therefore a member of a different new clan outside his

mother's house? Oedipus unknowingly kills his father—
that is the tragedy—and then returns to his mother's
womb, to his mother's clan. The effect of the crime is that
the matrilineal line is retained, because when Jocasta dies
and Oedipus goes into exile, a blind man, the power is
transferred to a man of her own clan, her brother, Creon.

Interpreted in this way, the tragedy of Oedipus is an
epic tale of a failed transition from the matrilineal system
to a patriarchal society. The desire to stay with the mother
and the hidden loyalty to the mother, is the unconscious
motive for the parricide.

I suspect that the reader has a few comments to make by
now with regard to hidden loyalties in the modern world,
starting with the traditional jokes about mothers-in-law.
The first contacts between a potential sexual couple and
between the families (clans) of this couple often take place
at mealtimes—sharing food together. It is a well-known
phenomenon that when a man marries, he goes into his
mother-in-law's family. He changes clan. It is equally common that when a woman marries, her loyalty continues to
belong to her original family, to her own mother. Her clan
remains the same. Every son/husband is soon confronted
with this phenomenon and with the explicit 'choice' that it
entails. The quotation marks indicate the extremely relative character of this notion of choice, because the direction of the choice is usually predetermined, in favour of
the woman. It is an equally well-known phenomenon that
this kind of choice has a particular effect at the difficult
point when an inheritance is divided—as a last expression
of the division of food. Any lawyer will confirm that the
problems arising from the division of goods are almost
always caused by the in-laws, the other clan, which insists
on its rights.

In the first instance, the tragedy of *Oedipus* can be read as a story of the transition from the matrilineal system to a patriarchal system, in the sense of a failed transition with a return to the previous stage. For a successful transition, we can look at another tragedy, *The Oresteia* by Aeschylus, a trilogy that describes an enormous change in human history.

The first part, *Agamemnon*, dates wholly from before this transition. On his way to Troy, Agamemnon has to make a sacrifice for a safe crossing over the sea. He sacrifices Iphigeneia, his own daughter. When he returns after his conquest of Troy, he is murdered by his wife Clytemnestra, (Iphigeneia's mother), and her lover. Thus, in the first part, the events all follow the rules of the matrilineal system. From the point of view of Clytemnestra, the murder of Agamemnon is not a crime, but just revenge. After all, Agamemnon does not belong to her clan, even though her daughter did. Using the same argument, the sacrifice of Iphigeneia is not a crime for Agamemnon, because she does not belong to his clan and his loyalties also lie elsewhere.

The place of the daughter is clear; she belongs to the mother's clan. The conflict of loyalties arises only with the son, Orestes, who has to make a choice. If he chooses his mother's clan, he abandons his loyalty to his father and automatically condones the murder of Agamemnon. If he takes his father's part, his loyalties will dictate that he take revenge and kill his mother. This conflict is the core of the second part, the *Choephori*('Bearers of the sacrifices for the dead'). Orestes chooses his father and kills his mother. As a result, the three Erinyes, the female goddesses of vengeance, are sent to pursue him. They persecute him, and in their turn take revenge from the matrilineal point of view.

The third part, the *Eumenides* (the 'well-intentioned ones') contains a judgement on the question of guilt. Orestes is supported by Apollo, the ultimate male god. There is a judgement in which he must be found guilty or innocent. The gods cast equal votes, and Athena, a goddess born only from a father, Zeus, casts the deciding vote. She pronounces him innocent, and thus Orestes is the only protagonist to survive the tragedies. Moreover, he survives without guilt. The goddesses of vengeance have to accept this decision and change into the Eumenides, kindly deities.

A remarkable aspect of the decision is contained in the words of Apollo, the male God, and Athena, the goddess born from a god (Zeus) without the intervention of a woman. The chorus—a group of women—asks Apollo to account for the plea he has put forward on behalf of Orestes. His response (*Eumenides*, verses 655-665), is unequivocal and places the loyalty wholly with the father:

This too I answer; mark the truth of what I say:
The mother is not the true parent of the child
Which is called hers. She is a nurse who tends the growth
Of young seed planted by its true parent, the male.
So, if Fate spares the child, she keeps it, as one might
Keep for some friend a growing plant. And of this truth,
That father without mother may beget, we have
Present, as proof, the daughter of Olympian Zeus:
One never nursed in the dark cradle of the womb;
Yet such a being no god will beget again.

103

This could not be clearer. The child is separated from the mother and henceforth belongs to the father, so that the former roles have been completely reversed. This also means that loyalties come to lie elsewhere, as we see in the reasons given by Pallas Athena when she has to cast the deciding vote (verses 734 ff.). The same significant development concludes the tragedy when the goddesses of vengeance have to be appeased. Characteristically for the conclusion, the chorus of *women* starts its interventions several times with the following complaint (verses 776-790):

The old is trampled by the new!
Curse on you younger gods who override
The ancient laws and rob me of my due!
Now to appease the honour you reviled
Vengeance shall fester till my full heart pours
Over this land on every side
Anger for insult, poison for my pain—
Yes, poison from whose killing rain
A sterile blight shall creep on plant and child
And pock the earth's face with infectious sores.
Why should I weep? Hear, Justice, what I do!
Soon Athens in despair shall rue
Her rashness and her mockery.
Daughters of Night and Sorrow, come with me,
Feed on dishonour, on revenge to be!

In the rest of the dialogue Pallas Athena recognises their wisdom, together with the fact that they are the elders, but at the same time tells them that they must submit to the decision. The transition to the patriarchal system is marked by the transformation of the female *Erinyes*, the goddesses of vengeance, to the female *Eumenides*, kindly deities who must guard the city from underneath the earth. In other words: mother earth.

The impossible centre of a discursive field

A self-made myth; anthropological excavation of kinships from a very remote past; classical tragedies; recent socio-cultural evolutions . . . The reconstruction of all these can never be on a factual basis—indeed, quite the contrary. The reconstruction always says a great deal more about our own time than it does about the past. Each interpretation of history takes place as a function of the present—and this applies to both collective and personal histories—although this does not prevent us from believing our history.

The quotations above are taken from what is now known as a discursive field. This refers to an open and loosely related collection of stories, each of which in its own way expresses a truth that is in itself intangible. Thus such a truth is felt rather than formulated, and feeling it in this way is always related to the same phenomenon—change. We feel the end of a season in our bones, together with the start of the new one. The precise nature of this change can only be guessed at, since it is based on limited observations.

In the distant past, we moved towards a patriarchal, monotheistic society. The children of a group of mothers inherited and bore the name of one father, which meant above all that they were removed from the mother. In the first instance this applied to the son, because the daughter became a mother herself and was therefore automatically in the other position. Therefore the original prohibition concerned the mother-son relationship and focused primarily on the mother, who was forbidden to harvest the fruit of her body. In this way, an original fear dating from a previous era was averted and developed a different guise in the next period. In its wake, diametrically opposed role patterns developed, as well as a gender identity, which acquired a self-fulfilling character. The whole system was supported and organised against a background of a belief in a divine father.

When the season changes, you can feel it in your bones. The question is whether it is only a change in the seasons, and therefore a circular movement with a predictable return to the same situation. It is also possible that there is a shift in the climate.

Orestes in the twentieth century, or nothing new under the sun

At the very least, we can come to the following conclusion from the above: that there have been some fundamental changes in the way human society is organised. If these changes are described only in terms of a switching of power between men and women, this ignores the fact that the contrast between men and women is itself the result of that evolution. The present form cannot possibly be found in the past.

Confronted with these shifts that took place over thousands of years, the question about the change itself also arises, particularly at the level of the individual psyche. In other words, do the changes that took place at a broader social level correspond to similar changes at an individual level? This question can be answered in two entirely different ways. On the one hand, we could assume that the human being has always remained fundamentally the same, and that any changes are merely arbitrary and do not affect the essential human character in any way. On the other hand, there is the diametrically opposed view that changes are possible and that the human being as such has already altered.

When we are confronted with these two alternatives and are asked to make a choice between them, the chances are that we almost automatically opt for the first alternative, that of the unchanging nature of the human being. Subsequently, we would probably make the distinction between essence and appearance, potentiality and act, matter and form. To put it more clearly, we might say that the changes visible in history can be reduced to insignificant external appearances, while the assumed inner essence remains unchanged. As Vandenberg wrote in his theory of changes, 'Continuity is the fruit of homogeneity obtained as a result of strong reduction'.

This line of thought is the rule rather than the exception, and it was adopted by Freud, among others. A similar argument allowed him to analyse Leonardo da Vinci as though he were a contemporary. This idea tallies perfectly with the general view of science, inspired by Darwin, that applied in the first half of our century. This view can be formulated as follows: there has certainly been change, but it takes place so infinitely slowly, and on a time scale so different from our own, that, to all intents and purposes, we live in an unchanging world. It is precisely because of this assumption that Freud had to go back to mythical primeval times situated between the ice ages, or perhaps even earlier, for the basis of the Oedipus complex, with his story about the so-called primal father and primal murder. The complex has existed along the same lines since that time.

It is actually an almost automatic reflex to opt for the first choice, that of an unchanging human nature, the 'nothing new under the sun' theory. From the scientific point of view, this has been part of our western pattern of thought since the time of Plato. We are always in search of eternal ideas, constants independent of time, place and person. Every tree must be traced back to the prototype of 'Tree', and something that has existed for centuries acquires status and significance simply as a result of this. The pre-Socratic idea of Heraclitus, 'Everything flows, nothing stays the same', belongs to the distant past. On the basis of this expectation of things staying the same, we can identify the Oedipus complex and the western family everywhere and at all times, from the Papuans to the Middle Ages. Even in *The Simpsons* there is a mother and a father . . . The fact that we have to make all sorts of changes and adaptations in this process of identification does not seem to bother us. After all, we maintain, *essentially* there are no differences. What is gained from recognising this sameness is not difficult to define—it creates an identifiable, predictable world in which the fear of the unknown is reduced to a minimum.

Meanwhile, we are blind to the changes which have taken place even in the short term. Norbert Elias convincingly demonstrated that there have been some far-reaching changes in relationships and rules in the last five hundred years. When his historical-sociological study, *The Civilizing Process*—first printed in 1939—was reprinted yet again in 1969, he considered that it was high time to write an introduction criticising his sociologist colleagues and challenging their blindness to these changes. The concept of invariables is merely a consequence of our way of thinking, and no more.

When we opt for the opposite view, namely that society and the individual are constantly subject to a continuous process of change, the question arises: what has changed with regard to the family? The triad of mother, child and father? And, related to this, male and female identity? In concrete terms, one might actually ask what changes there have been since the turn of the century. In this respect, we assume that the family is the channel for reciprocal influences between society and the individual, with the result that changes at one level have an effect on the other, and vice versa.

Once we abandon the idea of an unchanging human nature we are confronted with one surprise after another. A comparison of families nowadays with those of a century ago leads us to wonder whether we are really talking about the same thing at all. With only slight exaggeration, it may be said that the terms used are just about the only surviving point of correspondence. In the last hundred years, virtually all the functions—succinctly summarised in the triad of birth, sex and death—which used to constitute the essence of the family, have been moved outside it.

First, the process of growing up. In the past, a child basically grew up at home in a relatively limited social environment, while it is now often the case that babies and toddlers are cared for in day-care centres outside the family. Looking at the length of time as a criterion, a child is brought up almost entirely outside the family nowadays. Of the few hours spent in the family home, a large number are spent in front of the television, which has in several respects taken over the role of 'bringing up' the child.

Second, the care of the elderly and the sick. This takes us to the other side of the continuum from birth to death. Almost all of Freud and Breuer's patients in *Studies on Hysteria* became ill and suffered from stress themselves when they looked after their sick father or mother at home for weeks at a time. One of the subsidiary effects of this caring function was to highlight the difference between the generations: the younger, healthy generation compared with the older, sicker generation. Nowadays, both this function and the distinction have virtually disappeared. There is a universal myth of eternal youth and absence of sickness, which is illustrated in advertisements representing mother and daughter as two sisters.

Third, sexuality between the two previous extremes. While the family served in the past to provide a permanent sexual partner with all sorts of moral restrictions and the well-known double standard, this has now been replaced by what is described in the modern expression as 'serial monogamy'. Apart from the fear of AIDS and the resulting desire for a permanent partner, such an arrangement illustrates both a desire to form a couple and the failure to do so.

A fourth point, which seems to be unrelated at first sight, concerns eating. The family has its cultural and anthropological origins in the meal shared by the man and the woman. Therefore it is logical to see the death of the family at the point where they no longer eat together. Nowadays, this has also become the rule rather than the exception. Increasingly, people eat in front of the television, and the point at which the various members of the family meet most frequently is formed by the diagonal line between the fridge, the microwave and the goggle box.

It is a long distance between *The Simpsons* (1987)—who are still a family—and *Beavis and Butthead* (1993). Surely, it is no coincidence that Mike Judge (the spiritual 'father' of B & B) called them the 'bastard children of the sexual revolution'. He added that he knew them quite well, and that he attended the same school. In the even more recent *South Park* (1997) families are depicted as a sexually transmissible disease from which there is no escape. The tremendous success of these three cartoon series says a lot more about contemporary feelings on family life than any sociological survey.

This brief summary enables us at least to conclude that the family nowadays is very different from the family in the past. When the statistics on divorces and one-parent families are added to this, it becomes clear that it is even possible to question the existence of the family as such. Certainly it is so different that we can justifiably ask whether we are still talking about the same thing. It is inconceivable that this would not have any effect at an individual level. Undoubtedly, one result is that we are more individual than we have ever been in history. The material expression of this is literally visible architecture: everyone who can afford it has his own room, something that was quite inconceivable two generations ago. Moreover, this room is not just a bedroom but is furnished from primary school age on, as a private apartment, preferably with its own television and a computer. We merely have to join the Internet and the door can remain entirely closed.

The main shift encompassing all the previous cases is not quite so easy to identify, though it forms the basis for all the other changes. This concerns the function of *authority*. I would like to stress the difference between authority, fatherhood, and—by extension—the function of the father. Authority is *not* synonymous with power. In fact, I would even argue that power is directed *against* authority, because authority is only an operational element in a particular process. This is the process of *separation*.

In my view, it is separation which is essential to becoming a human being. Separation constitutes one end of a continuum which has *union* at its other end. Every human

being can (indeed, must) abandon his original 'unity'—
with mother, the nuclear family, or subgroup of a clan—in
order to effect a new union, elsewhere, with a new and different group. This is brought about on the basis of an
authoritarian intervention. In the first essay, I regarded
this intervention as the prohibition on incest, the command that one has to marry outside the nuclear family,
which thus establishes the foundations of culture and of
all human production. Within a patriarchal society, then,
separation is a function exercised through the figure of the
father. However, in this second essay we have seen that
separation and fathers are not an inevitable combination,
because the rules of separation existed long before there
was any question of fathers or fatherhood. Within the
clans, separation took place according to the rules of
taboos on food and—later—on sexuality. On the basis of
these rules, identifiable groups developed which could
organise exchanges. The separation from the first group
was always accompanied by the entrance into another
union, resulting in a sociocultural perpetual motion.

Considered in these terms, the goal of separation as
such is essential, and its link with fatherhood and patriarchy is secondary. From a psychoanalytic point of view,
the underlying dynamics can be understood in terms of
jouissance. By putting distance between one group or figure and another, or by imposing a new union, the whole
process boils down to a redistribution of jouissance. In this
way, a collective restriction is established by the authority
of the group, which sets down this authority in a symbolic form—from mythical tales to legal texts.

Historically, the function of separation has become
increasingly ascribed to a single figure—the father—and
increasingly viewed as taking place in relation to another
figure—the mother. Yet, as an actual person, the individual

father can exercise this function and its related authority only on the basis of an underlying symbolic structure—in this case, the patriarchal monotheistic system of which he has become the representative. Formally speaking, there is not much difference here from the clan system, in the sense that a child is still separated from one family group to become part of another. The process is achieved when the father's name is bestowed upon the child. The evolution from the clan system to the patriarchal family introduced also a shift in the object of pleasure: from food to sexuality, although the two still cross over into one another, even today. Cultures with a sophisticated cuisine usually also have sophisticated erotic tastes, and vice versa.

Recent history demonstrates that groups established in this way are becoming smaller and smaller, shrinking from the original, extensive patriarchal family towards the modern nuclear family. Along with this shift the individual becomes increasingly more individual, and the ego reigns triumphant. In modern times, the function of separation has evolved as far as it can, and the result is a boomerang effect—the individual is not only separated from the first group, but also from the first 'Other'. He is actually separated from virtually any form of social link, without being able to enter into a new union. The era of egocracy and egology has arrived.

This shift forms part of a major change concerning authority and power. In the past, there were collectively accepted and ratified rules and norms to regulate the distribution of pleasure (food, sexuality). These were derived from similarly collective conventions, usually embedded in a broader context—religion, ideology, legislation, science. Nowadays, these group rules are increasingly rejected and are being replaced by individual arrangements ('rule'

113

would be too strong a term here) between two unique individuals. This explains the increasingly familiar terms 'mutual consent' and 'informed consent'; any pleasure is permitted, as long as there is reciprocal agreement. However, it is my suspicion that this kind of agreement, due to the lack of an authority, is usually enforced by power. The only point on which collective agreement is still required is regarding the age at which someone is able to give this 'informed consent'. In other words: from what age is sexuality permitted, and from what age is sexual activity no longer paedophilia?

Two recent phenomena are characteristic of this evolution. An examination of a current book on psychopathology and a comparison with one from about fifteen years ago shows that a number of categories have disappeared from the recent version. It is not that these no longer exist, far from it; the change lies in the way in which they are evaluated. The most striking difference concerns homosexuality. In the past, this was considered a perversion, a deviation to be feared, but now there is a political pressure group, and therefore it is normal. It is predictable that a number of other categories will follow: transvestism, bisexuality, transsexuality. The changing terms for these phenomena are also typical. The term 'perversion' is now politically incorrect, and has been replaced by 'paraphilia', which appears alongside 'normophilia'. The problem is that it is no longer at all clear *which norm* should be considered the norm. A second illustration can be found in the recent legal wranglings about SM couples whose sexual practices have suddenly been publicised for some reason and have become a matter of complaint. The arguments in these proceedings clearly take the following line—are adults acting with mutual consent able to make their own arrangements with regard to sexual pleasure, or are they subject to a group norm? Quite apart from the legal implications, it is particularly important to see that, only twenty years ago, this question itself would have been quite inconceivable.

A development of this kind can be assessed in very different ways, from a positive assessment—more freedom and individual rights of decision-making, to a negative one—the decay of morality and the loss of group consciousness. Beyond these moral—and therefore always arbitrary—considerations, one thing is clear: the repercussions on formerly collectively accepted authority and on the father as a representative of this collectivity, are visible everywhere. The far-reaching degree of separation also separates the child from the father, who therefore loses his position and consequently his authority. In fact, even when he wants to exercise this authority, there is an immediate suspicion that he is interested only in his own pleasure. Authority prevails as long as its power does not have to be invoked. The former patriarchal authority has now broken down on every front. Not only is the emperor wearing no clothes, he is guilty.

This is why every form of power has become suspect in the second half of our century. While it was implicitly assumed in the past that an authority represented a higher ideal, and that the exercise of this authority was aimed solely at achieving this ideal, it is now assumed that someone with power is interested only in his own profit, that is, in his own pleasure. Politicians, industrialists and spiritual leaders are all viewed in the same way, and the tidal wave of complaints is unstoppable. The same applies to fathers, who in the last decade have all become guilty of potential incest. In the past, parents were contacted by schools because their children had been naughty. Now parents are contacted by schools because the mother's partner cannot keep his hands off the children.

This is echoed in the sensational media by a general climate of fear and confusion. As a result, a modern myth has developed, the idea that everything was much better in the past, in the good old days. People forget that the traditional family in the period after the industrial revolution was probably one of the most cruel social institutions in recent history. Nevertheless, fear and confusion prevail. The effect of this at the level of the individual is predictable—he starts looking for old securities. In itself, there is nothing new in this. It is what I referred to above as the 'traditional' solution. History is full of illustrations, and in this respect there have been plenty of unfortunate repetitions.

Should we expect the same evolution yet again? I believe not, because a different gender relationship is forming. I believe that the traditional solution has become impossible, because the basis for it has disappeared—that is, the patriarchal-monotheistic complex. Nevertheless, this does not mean that there are no efforts directed towards this solution—indeed they are all around us. However, in the age of information these solutions display one big difference. Whereas the traditional solution, in the past, always amounted to a new interpretation of the same symbolically supported master function in which religious and ideological systems alternated, these days the symbolic authority function itself has disappeared. Consequently, any solution based on this line of thought inevitably results in the establishment of crude, unnegotiated power figures. In other words, primal fathers.

Primal fathers, Incorporated

The psychological environment in which our great-grand-parents grew up was extremely restricted. The main anchor figures were their own parents, and possibly any living grandparents. In addition, there were neighbours and a small number of figures of reference (the doctor, the mayor, the school teacher and so forth). At best, there were a few additional models for identification taken from books that were read on long winter evenings.

The identity of someone who grew up in this world can be defined as a limited and divided entity. There is a division, because every child is inevitably faced with different and often contradictory desires, in the confrontation with two, and only two, central identification figures—father and mother. It is restricted because there are only two figures. This duality is reflected in the main mechanisms involved in the development of such an identity, namely, identification and repression. On closer examination, these appear to be two aspects of the same process, identification revealing the conscious upper side, while repression provides the refused underside.

In this sort of restricted environment, the division remains relatively stable because it develops within the boundaries of the Oedipal scene, with the child between the father and the mother. The result is that the psyche is viewed by Freud as a split entity, with the idea of conflict within this duality being of central importance. Of course, the best known expression of this duality is the division between consciousness and the unconscious. For example, a symptom—or in broader terms, a neurosis—is always a compromise solution between two opposing desires, one of which must come off worse, opposing desires that almost always lead back to the parental couple: *'Who do you love most, mummy or daddy?'* The conscious, visible part of the duality has developed by means of identification, while the unconscious part has developed as a result of repression. After Freud, this idea of division recurs in virtually every psychological theory, albeit in different terms: the true self opposed to the false self, the Parent versus the Child, conflicts of loyalties, double bind, and the like.

The modern environment is radically different. The importance of the parents nowadays is only a fraction of what it used to be, and from the very beginning there are numerous reference figures in an ever-faster changing series of nannies, baby-sitters, teachers, mummy's latest boyfriend, daddy's latest girlfriend, and new neighbours. Television produces a never-ending stream of images ensuring that virtual reality is more real than real reality, which in turn is not merely a pale reflection of this, but in many cases even becomes a product of it. A modern identity can no longer be described in terms of the Freudian divided duality. Instead the idea of *division* has a central place. The modern individual has developed in a much less stable environment, with an enormous supply of figures to identify with, all of whom have their own contribution to make. How many of these figures has a modern ten-year-old come across in his life, compared with his predecessor in 1905? The early Freudian identification has now been replaced by Lacanian alienation, in which the subject is turning on a wheel of a never-ending succession of reference figures, constantly divided by different desires. The predictable effect of this is the often desperate search for a point of security that will provide an anchor for the subject so that he can achieve a recognisable identity. The more someone becomes divided, the more he searches for something to identify with, even if it is only an extremely banal member of a football team or a particular brand of clothing. In the past, these anchors always had a dual nature because of the dual structure of the identification: you were a woman or a man, a father or a mother, a child or a parent, and so on. The modern anchor points have exploded in the continuous movement of the wheel. You are no longer a boy or a girl, but a Tristan or Charlotte, a mod, surfer, straight-edger, hard rocker, new ager. In the absence of a central identification figure, the so-called 'peer group' has become increasingly important. Each of these groups ultimately becomes the source of new norms or conventions that develop almost unnoticed, not borne by a single individual, but by all the members—the peers. There is a new clan structure in the making.

Not everyone is part of such a peer group. The desire for a secure anchor has resulted in the fact that people today can be described as being hysterical by definition. In this sense, hysteria means being divided among a multitude of desires that always come from outside and are therefore alienating. It results in a search for a unifying factor that will serve as a guarantee. Modern hysteria is looking for an Other as a place of safety, looking for something or someone in whom to *believe*.

Belief has become a dirty word belonging to a distant past, dating from the days before science and the scepticism that science entails. This applies only to the extent that the view is restricted to traditional religious beliefs. A broader view shows that the postmodernist is very much a believer, with beliefs aimed at quieting the constant gnawing doubts present in the background. Have I chosen the right profession? And the right partner? Am I eating healthy food? Am I making love in the best way? Answers to these questions, together with a confirmation that they are right, are sought from the Other, from macrobiotics to

New Age, to the latest form of psychoanalysis: 'Lacan said that . . .'.

Paradoxically, this view is concealed behind a much more striking characteristic: the fact that hysteria greatly undermines and questions authority, and particularly authority believed in by other people. An hysterical subject is the ultimate zealot, always ready to attack another religion, ideology or football team in the name of his or her own belief, which is seen as the only true belief. This conflict can assume truly violent forms in a confrontation between two very similar—and therefore rival—belief systems. In this respect, reality often transcends caricature; there is a taste of this in the Monty Python film, *Life of Brian*. The story is set at the time of Christ, and depicts, amongst other things, the Jewish resistance to the Roman occupying forces. When he has penetrated into the dungeons of the Roman palace, a member of the People's Front of Judea shouts: 'The enemy!' to which his fellow soldier asks: 'The Romans?' The indignant answer is: 'No, a bastard from the Judea People's Front':

- *'The only people we hate more than the Romans, are the fucking Judea People's Front. And the Judea Popular People's Front and the People's Front of Judea.'*
- *'But we are the People's Front of Judea!'*
- *'I thought we were the Popular Front... People's Front!'*

It is the rule rather than the exception for an hysterical subject, while searching for the one and only real truth, the ultimate guarantee, to meet up with a figure who guarantees 'The Truth' on the basis of his or her specific personality structure. The content of this truth is of subordinate importance, because its credibility is entirely related to this personality structure. This latter is best described as being

120

diametrically opposed to that of the hysteric. Constantly torn and full of inner doubt, the hysteric is fascinated by a figure with a massive sense of self-assurance who knows it all, and who pronounces this knowledge like an oracle, without the slightest sign of any inner doubt.

In psychiatry, this is referred to as a paranoid personality, not to be confused with an overt paranoid psychosis. The latter condition should be seen rather as a failure, the failure of the paranoid personality as such. We will not explore the reasons for the development of the paranoid personality, or of its possible failure. Suffice it to say, the last word has not yet been uttered on the subject. However, there is a lot of agreement about its characteristics. The paranoid personality is a man in one piece. He knows, and he knows that he knows. This knowledge assumes the form of a self-confirming system that provides answers for typically existential questions. How should you be a man? How should you be a woman? What is the relationship between the two? What is the role of children? In other words, the System will always have the right answer in any matter relating to the distribution of pleasure. In psychiatric terms, this gives rise to a typical style of delusions, particularly megalomania, the delusion of grandeur characterised by the absence of any doubt or self-reflection, with only massive self-assurance remaining. Any defect or shortcoming is always and inevitably attributed to another person, with the consequence that the paranoid personality becomes innocence personified. Not only is he innocent, he is also convinced of the continuous malevolence of others who are out to get him, plotting against him and even persecuting him. This last characteristic is so striking that paranoia and delusions of persecution have become almost synonymous, although the latter is only a characteristic, and not the essence of this condition. The essence lies rather in the fact that this personality is in no way divided, in stark contrast to the fragmented personality of the hysteric.

A comparison between an hysterical subject and a paranoid personality reveals how the problem of the one is in each case solved by that of the other. The problem of the paranoid personality is that the condition of omniscience is fairly fragile, as long as he is the only one convinced of this undivided knowledge. The result is that he must convince others, and this is why so many paranoid personalities start to write or preach from the pulpit. They need an audience, who then form a group of unconditional followers confirming the status of omniscience, precisely because of their unconditional support. The hysterically divided subject is in search of a master figure with no shortcomings, who can guarantee the correct answers and in this way absolve him from the pain of division. An encounter with a paranoid personality is usually a success, particularly because it also entails an encounter with a group in which the hysterical subject can lose his own inner divisions.

There are numerous examples of this in the modern world, from gang leaders to sex gurus, to political pundits, each with their own groupies. It is a relationship that has always existed, but it flourishes in particularly rich soil nowadays because of the above-mentioned social developments.

Credo quia absurdum: 'I believe this because it makes no sense'

This process is the same one that underlies a particular sort of group formation, one that is typical of male hierarchical groups such as the church and the army. The leader assumes the position of the ego ideal, and all the members identify with him. This common identification removes their original divisions and also ensures that the group members start to resemble each other, especially through the development of a similar way of speaking, which in turn reveals a like-minded way of thinking.

There was a time when the first such group was the family, with the father in the function of the ego ideal. Identifying with him resulted in a more or less recognisable family identity through the development of a common superego. This is much the same as an ego ideal, though the emphasis is more on what is forbidden. The content of the superego was determined by the rules that applied in the broader social group. The paternal function amounted to the representation of this social authority, which was, in turn, based on a collectively accepted belief system.

This mainly symbolic function was effective in the sense that it gave the developing subject the opportunity to put an end to the inner divisions related to desire and pleasure by identifying with the norms of someone who was placed in the master position. This identification was then broken down at characteristic moments of development—puberty and adolescence, the rules of the father were thrown overboard and the subject's own norms were developed. This is the normal evolution of what could be called a normal developmental hysteria: the creation of, and belief in, an omnipotent father in childhood, the challenge and destruction of this figure during puberty, and a more nuanced and integrated position during adulthood.

It now looks as though this former, literally 'self-evident', normal evolution is disappearing. A closer examination of why it is disappearing brings us to the distinction between the function and the real figure. No father can embody the function of undivided guarantor as regards desires and pleasure, because he too is divided, at least between his father and his mother. At most, he can assume this function as a conduit, a semi-permeable membrane that allows group convictions to seep through. This conviction is then guaranteed by the group—it is true because we all believe in it. The result of this is predictable. The moment the group itself starts to doubt the belief, there is a sense of restlessness and a search for new answers. The developmental hysteria then becomes stuck at a certain point and assumes an almost permanent form, with the typical symptom of loss of meaning and the impossibility of creating such a meaning oneself. The creation of meaning is a group product.[4]

The decay of the authority function can therefore be traced back to the disintegration of the group conviction. Thus, on a wider scale, we see an evolution taking place within groups similar to that which occurs in individuals. For centuries there was at most a collective division into two halves, so that one group conviction predominated in a way that was regularly confirmed by oppressing a smaller dissident group. The main reason why the Christians needed the Saracens was to strengthen their own convictions, and the same happened on a larger scale with the Reformation and the emergence of Protestantism. This contrast set the scene for a clearly defined identity, and therefore for stability. You were for or against, black or white. From the time that there were no longer two or three convictions but a wave of new 'truths', the possibility of developing a clear identity disappeared and uncertainty increased—what to choose, whom to believe?

Seen in this light, the authority of the father at the beginning of this century was the effect of a massive shared religious conviction, which always amounted to a patriarchal monotheism, no matter how differently this was expressed at different times and places. The effect of and the need for such a conviction can be measured most accurately in what was presumed to be a liberation from the religious yoke, namely the emergence of more or less scientifically founded ideologies. Russian communism, based on the dialectical materialism of Marx, swept Papa Tsar and the Orthodox Church from the table in one movement and installed equality among all comrades. A quarter of a century later, however, they needed Papa Stalin to restrain the by now intolerable splits. The same thing has been repeated again and again throughout this century (Hitler, Mao, Khomeni, Saddam . . .)—a new figure sweeps aside an old regime in the name of a new truth, only to install the same structure as before, albeit in an even worse form.

The rapid alternation among these different ideologies, combined with the similar ways in which they failed, has led to a virtual disappearance of a belief in 'the' system in our century. Of the *Credo quia absurdum* we have retained above all the *absurdum,* with post-modern cynicism as its exponent. A book such as Sloterdijk's *Critique of Cynical Reason* was literally inconceivable a hundred years ago, but it now expresses a general feeling. There is no longer a great Other who is still credible.

This applies all the more because the longed for 'deliverance from religion' movement has failed. Since the Enlightenment, there has been a growing hope that Science, in its modern form, would provide all the right answers so that it would be possible to abandon religion as something belonging to a previous era. There was some reason for this hope: the biblical story of the Creation was replaced by Lyell and Darwin, medicine advanced by

125

leaps and bounds, and Jules Verne formulated the mechanical dreams of a society that had only just discovered machines and industry. It was to be expected that this science would be able to answer the old questions that had been answered by religion in the past.

These hopes were not fulfilled. On the contrary, the opposite happened because the initial euphoria about the great new discoveries was followed by a period in which science was concerned with 'falsification', that is, the scientific proof that something is *not* correct, so that the mountain of uncertainties continued to grow. Nowadays it is enough for an expert to attend a conference in his or her own specialist field and go back home burdened with new doubts. As a result, the modern intellectual has turned into the temporary reincarnation of Hamlet, always doubting before going into action, weighing up arguments for and against so that every choice is neutralised. Meanwhile, he is trampled by those who are not hampered by a surfeit of knowledge and intelligence.

The 'will to knowledge', eroticism and monsters [5]

The position that had been abandoned by religion and refused by science was initially filled by the ideological systems described above. Each called on science in its own way, but ultimately appeared to be more related to the opium that they sought to oppose. The fact that various different systems of this kind arose during one century reveals a number of common characteristics. For example, it is very striking that they cannot function without a central figure, thus immediately exposing their similarity to patriarchal monotheism. The common characteristic of these figures is not only their despotic exercise of power, but also, and above all, the fact that each of them exercises this power on the basis of a presumed *knowledge* that can be recognised in writings and texts written either by them or by others: *Das Kapital, Mein Kampf,* the little red or yellow book. In other words, a bible, with the understanding that even the Bible is only a bible. Once again this confirms the relationship between *homo hystericus* and the paranoid personality described above. The texts, no matter how much their content may differ, provide answers to the question that science could not answer: how should life be lived? Above all, it provides answers to a number of delicate questions—who or what determines authority, what is the right attitude to pleasure, what is the relationship between the two sexes, or to put it in more precise terms, what is the position of the woman? As regards this last question, no matter how differently it is answered, the answer is always the same: underneath. In such a system, the woman must be dominated and the danger that she represents must be curbed, even before it has been identified.

The fact that the search for this knowledge goes on all the time, together with a search for guarantees, confronts us with what is probably the basic reason driving man to seek knowledge—the wish to know about sexuality. It is no coincidence that Michel Foucault entitled the first part of his history of sexuality *La Volonté de Savoir* ('The Will to Knowledge'). Human beings are looking for answers in this field. The child's first investigations are focused on so-called games of 'doctors and nurses', and so are his first theories, the so-called 'infantile sexual theories': what is the difference between me and the other sex, where do children come from, what is the relationship between my father and my mother? This need to know becomes even more powerful when established cultural answers have lost their credibility. Here we have a reason for an almost essential combination. A figure who wishes to dominate a broad social group must, as a master, produce a theory and knowledge to answer the most basic questions.

This knowledge has been drawn up and guaranteed by the master. The link between knowledge and the master has an unexpected spin-off. Knowledge, particularly the exposition of knowledge, not only confers power but also has a very erotic effect. At the start of *The Grapes of Wrath*, John Steinbeck introduces a tragic figure, a preacher, who can no longer preach because he has too many doubts, but who remembers how he would successfully seduce his female followers after his thundering sermons. The tragedy lies in the divided nature of this figure, who looks back nostalgically at something he no longer wants, but still desires.

Even with a knowledge of history, the same erotic fascination still emanates from Hitler's speeches more than half a century after they were made. Mao's pronouncements were followed with bated breath by millions of Red Guards transported by his words, and Stalin's silences were always interpreted to show that he could say what he wanted, but chose not to. In a milder version, the same potential relationship can be found in every teaching situation, from the university professor to the skiing instructor. As soon as we think someone else knows it all, this has an erotic effect. The effect is multiplied a hundredfold when that person can also explain it well—every Don Juan is a good talker.

In itself, I believe this illustrates what I wrote at the end of the first essay. The relationship between men and women lies in the word—it is not only achieved there but actually created there. There are as many methods of creation as there are styles. In that essay we referred to only two forms, the poetic and the prosaic form. The form confronting us here is historically the most dangerous, the demagogic rhetorical form. It is this form that has gained the upper hand in our day, and has done so in an area that is not recognised.

The perverse superego: enjoy!

Traditionally this danger is expected from the major ideologies and their prophets. As soon as such a figure emerges somewhere and attracts followers, the quality newspapers are full of historical comparisons and warnings. The risks at this level seem fairly slight at this point in history. This is not so much because of the fact that we have learned anything from history, or as a result of these warnings, but because of the huge numbers of such figures. While in the past it was possible for one man to gain the attention of a whole nation, every nation is now divided among different figures, each of whom can attract only part of the whole. The universal trend towards unification today is mainly a reflection of the fragmentation which can be felt on every front, from European political union to the local football team.

Instead of the large system guaranteed by a single mythical figure, we are now in an era of minor, often rather pathetic little patriarchs, each with his own primal horde, which they fearfully guard and protect from the evil world outside.

The ongoing fragmentation that accompanies this entails protecting us from the danger of a totalitarian system in the political and ideological sense of the word. Only the future will tell whether this danger really has declined to any great extent. However, discussion of this phenomenon means that we may lose sight of another dimension. There already *is* a totalitarian system that is becoming increasingly global and imposing world-wide norms and rules on the relationship between men and women. Further, it is itself hardly bound by any rules, except those of economic success. This is the power of the media, with advertising in the lead, and taking the top place once assumed by Hollywood. Every ten-year-old can sing along with advertising slogans, dance to video clips and even dream pre-programmed images.

It is almost impossible to overestimate the influence this has. We have only to look at the budgets of the advertisers to realise what is at stake. Nowadays, the science and practice of psychology is no longer carried out in university laboratories. It is developed and improved in scores of marketing agencies that examine human differences in experiments unhampered by too many ethical considerations, with the aim of manipulating them as efficiently as possible. Meanwhile, academic psychologists continue to worry about the question of whether violence in children's films might or might not lead to real violence in the streets. 'Moose are frequently found in large numbers'etc!

It certainly isn't necessary to set up a large-scale study to find out that just about every advertising message is focused either on the relationship between men and women or on parent-child interaction. Questions that science cannot answer are constantly answered, displayed and described in this context. This confronts us with a strange phenomenon called 'reification'—the word creates the thing. If something is repeated often enough it starts to exist on the strength of this continued repetition. The desires, relationships and education shown in advertising messages thus become more and more real because they are presented, acted out and sung with unremitting monotony. Eventually, this reality is imposed.

A liberated, enlightened spirit might object that this danger is not in any way new. All this was prescribed in the past by the church or other ideologies, and it is now done by advertising. As a system there is little difference in a formal sense, because in each case something is imposed from outside and therefore involves a fundamentally alienating situation. The moral indignation of those frustrated people who bristle whenever a breast or buttock appears in a video clip or in an advertisement says more about their own censored desires. The fact that cars are sold using pin-ups and soft drinks by surfers wrestling each other has become part of our world. The danger is not in the lack of censorship or in the association of irrelevancies with sexuality. After all, *anything* can be erotic, and this is not the fault of advertising. On the contrary, the possibility of this association is actually a precondition for the existence of advertising. The cause of this lies in a characteristic of human desire that was described above—the fact that it can never be wholly fulfilled and therefore leads to constant movement.

Certainly, the alienating character of desires created in this way is not an argument against advertising, despite all the claims suggesting this. 'Advertising creates new needs', 'Advertising alienates people from their deepest desires'. No, as such, alienation has always existed. In his characteristic, ambiguous style, Lacan wrote: '*Le désir de l'homme, c'est le désir de l'Autre*' (Man's desire is the desire of and for the Other). Our desire always goes through that of another, starting with that of our parents and finishing with that of the latest object of our love. 'You have to follow your *own* desires' is an impossible task. Every so-

131

called 'own' desire relates to someone else, either in a positive or in a negative sense. It is only when you don't care that you don't desire.

Thus the danger posed by advertising and the media does not lie in the alienation they involve. It is connected with a particular aspect of the message of this new 'Other'. In the first essay I remarked that all earlier systems—whether religious or ideological—contain rules with regard to desire and pleasure. No matter how different these rules may be in different systems, they all have one feature in common—they entail a restriction. This is so transparently obvious that Michel Foucault elevated it to an essential characteristic in his historical treatise on sexuality. The rule—for ideology is too strong a term—expressed in advertising messages is in stark contrast to this. Briefly summarised: enjoy!

This is the new command of the superego—enjoy now, enjoy fully as long and as much as possible. The universal contemporary leitmotif is: *'Have it now.'* While religions promised happiness and tranquillity in the hereafter, and the ideologies promised this in a near post-revolutionary future, the contemporary message is what appeared on an ad for an aperitif: 'I want it right here, I want it right now'.

At first sight, the modern hedonist will not see any problem with this—on the contrary. What could be wrong with pleasure, except that it is not available to everyone in the same way for the time being?

Before becoming embroiled in an uninteresting moral discussion, it is important to unmask the messenger behind the media message. Compared to the situation in the past, in which the relationship between a paranoid personality and a hysterical group was outlined, the great difference is that in the case of media advertising there is

132

no personification in a figure of flesh and blood. Nevertheless, 'big brother' who is felt to be there beyond the messages of the advertisements, can still be identified. It is always a *perverse* 'big brother' who is consciously manipulating the group. The perverse aspect lies, among other things, in the fact that the advertisement gives the impression that it has the target group's best interests at heart and wants to inform them and tell them about the fantastic product they can buy, and about the new possibilities open to them. In fact, the only concern is to make a profit. This confronts us with the perverse father who gives the impression that he is concerned only with his children's welfare quite independently of any form of self-interest, but who is meanwhile carefully calculating his own pleasure—all at the expense of his children.

This is the paradox: there is less pleasure now than there ever was.

Father Christmases, who start appearing in mid-October, barely manage to attract any enthusiasm. During the ultimate buying week, the week of 'pure pleasure' at Christmas and New Year, the supermarkets are full of dull figures pushing laden trolleys, while a sickly sweet voice tries to tempt them even further. Wife-swapping during the post-Christmas period, combined with the latest model of vibrator, may just about break through this boredom for a moment, but meanwhile we are confronted, as regular as clockwork, with ever-increasing levels of aggression, in other words, fear. The message does not work. It requires further analysis.

The command shouted from the rooftops by the perverse father is diametrically opposed to that of the rules of the clan or the Oedipal father of the past. Their command was: not now and not here, but later, and somewhere else, so that there was room for a dimension of desire. This is the first consequence of the new superego morality: the 'right here, right now' kills desire with a surfeit of objects. It creates the illusion of a sort of voluntary materialism. Every desire can be stilled with an object that is for sale: all you have to do is make the decision and carry it out. This is the new alienating myth that seeps in everywhere nowadays, and is replacing the previous equally alienating myth. The previous myth was the Hollywood version of the couple who live happily ever after. I would call the present myth 'the junkie ideology'—buy the right stuff and pleasure follows. Meanwhile the fact that this is not the case has become increasingly clear. The main result is boredom and a search for new boundaries.

The latter element—a search for a new prohibition—reveals the importance of a curtailment of enjoyment. The original prohibition/command was the condition for the possibility of finding pleasure, albeit in a restricted way. This restriction was the source of frustration and complaints, and removing it was aimed at achieving limitless enjoyment, preferably for the largest possible number of people. It was a great surprise to find out that this was not the case. The unexpected result of the obligation to enjoy was summarised by Lacan in what he called 'Plus-de-jouir'. This untranslatable pun makes the link between constant increase in pleasure '(Plus, encore plus'), and the loss of pleasure ('plus de'). To cap it all, it is by no means rare to find that the (p)leisured classes are confronted with an even more unexpected effect on the way to this unrestricted enjoyment: anxiety.

Pleasure and anxiety are two sides of the same coin. The question arises whether the distinction is not primarily related to the way people interpret what they experience. If this interpretation goes in the direction of anxiety, the result is predictable: 'fight or flight'.

Meanwhile, we are no longer concerned with the aperitif, but with the figure beyond the object. Against this background, pleasure, anxiety and aggression will all be focused on woman who either has to be dominated or fled from. Woman stands for something very different, something unidentifiable, something real beyond any form of partial pleasure. When Zeus, after yet another quarrel with his wife, Hera, asks Tiresias who has the most enjoyment, the reply is that the woman has ten times as much pleasure as the man. It is from this figure that he flees.

The frightened band of heroes

Both historical anthropology and the great epic tales depict a peculiar phenomenon. Woman is seen as a threat to man which must be overcome. The monotheistic patriarchal system is the result of this never-ending attempt at domination. The success of this attempt gave rise to an ever greater contrast between men and women regarding gender identity. The specific way in which this contrast was expressed (strong-weak, etc) ensured that a constant factor became more and more hidden from history—fear of the woman. The current failure of the monotheistic patriarchal complex has two consequences. In the first place, this previously concealed fear is re-emerging in its entirety, this time with a number of predictable effects (flight/fight). Secondly, a positive result is that it is becoming increasingly clear that the traditional division between men and women should be abandoned to an ever-greater extent and make way for a much more differentiated gender identity.

This results in fear. The question is: why? It seems as though fear of women is an essential characteristic of men in the patriarchal system, something that exists by definition and can vary only in terms of intensity. Below, we will see that this fear goes back to a far older anxiety affecting both sexes, of which the male version is merely a specific sexualised form.

Anxiety is a basic affect. This means that in itself it cannot hide any other affect and, conversely, that all other emotions can be traced back to it. Aggression and hatred are the best known of these, but admiration and worship are also founded on fear. The position ascribed to the woman by the man is constantly fluctuating between these two extremes, hatred and love, but in both cases she remains an object of apprehension.

One of the cruellest, and at the same time strangest forms of aggression against women concerns institutionalised genital mutilation. In the 'lighter' version, the upper part of the clitoris is cut away. In the case of the full clitoridectomy, the whole clitoris, together with part of the labia minora, is removed. The most severe form is infibulation, which not only cuts away the entire female genitalia, but also sews up the remains of the labia majora. Historically these practices are associated with Muslim culture, but the custom is much older and more widespread. To associate it only with 'primitive' cultures is a big mistake. Clitoridectomy was practised in western Europe and the United States during the second half of the nineteenth century, albeit in a medical context.

It is difficult to find accurate data about the actual frequency of this phenomenon. The transition from a religious context to a pseudo-scientific one makes it even more surprising, and suggests that it is based on common grounds. These certainly exist. The mutilation is intended to destroy the woman's sexual enjoyment or rather, the form of female pleasure presumed and feared by the man. This already existed in the religious context, and the motive became even clearer in the case of medical interventions, which were invariably carried out to prevent presumed sexual perversions—from masturbation to hysteria to nymphomania. This actual removal of the physical source of female pleasure was replaced in the first half of the twentieth century by a scientific taboo. In the name of Freudian(!) science, only vaginal orgasm was permissible, and clitoral orgasm was decried as being bad, unfeminine, immature. In practice, this amounted to a prohibition on women actively experiencing pleasure.

These cruel actions not only indicate the level of the man's fear but also provide a kind of explanation. What is it that he must restrain, suppress, dominate and—when this proves to be impossible—what must he flee from? The answer lies in his interpretation of female enjoyment. The pleasure that the man presumes in the woman reduces him to a mere object, an instrument without a will, which is used and consumed. It is this unconscious and fearful fantasy that lies at the basis of a phenomenon very familiar to the modern woman. When she expresses her sexual desires too clearly, the modern Romeo takes flight. He has a headache, he is too tired, and so forth. The first confessions of men faking orgasms have now been recorded.

The Japanese film, *Empire of the Senses*, which was banned for a long time, fully reveals this fear. A young woman consumes a man down to the bone, to the point where he is reduced to a quivering mass of flesh. The film is unbearable because the images try to reveal the furthest

extent of the male fantasy and the related fear of the pleasure that he presumes in the woman.

What the man fears is the transgression, the crossing of
a boundary beyond which he will cease to exist. The
woman, merely by being a woman, invites him to go right
up to this boundary and awakens in him a need to cross
this limit. Every woman opens the abyss into which the
man fears/desires to fall. Camille Paglia formulated this
relationship most succinctly in a book that exploded like a
bomb within the politically correct feminist culture of
America. In her argument, nature/woman is opposed to
culture/man in an eternal struggle:

> For the male, every act of intercourse is a return to
> the mother and a capitulation to her. For men, sex is
> a struggle for identity. In sex, the male is consumed
> and released again by the toothed power that bore
> him, the female dragon of nature. (Paglia 1990, 13-
> 14)

Sex is a struggle that the man always loses, but he constantly enters the fray again, driven by an inner force that
he does not recognise in himself and that he therefore
places outside himself, with the woman. He either fights it
or flees from it, but either way, it is at her expense.

It is striking that the woman herself does not have, or
barely has, this fear of sexualised transgression. This is
probably one of the reasons why classical psychoanalysis
assumed that women had fewer feelings of guilt or a less
developed superego than their male partners. It was not
yet realised that these feelings of guilt lay elsewhere, in her
relation to her children.

Transgression in experiencing pleasure, where there is a risk of crossing a particular boundary, takes the male to the point of ultimate fear—the point at which he disappears. The fact that this is the ultimate form is clear from the way in which it is manifested in the consulting room. Two forms of fear can be outlined—a primary form, so far as it is unprocessed and unmediated, and a secondary form that makes the first kind acceptable. The latter is known as phobia, where a secondary object or situation is wrongly linked to the original fear. In this case, the therapy consists in disconnecting it, so that the secondary situation can be made free of fear.

The study of the original anxiety is difficult, precisely because it is almost impossible to name—it is always the secondary phobia that provides a description, and therefore a handle for it. If the therapist insists, he is told something in the sense of a fear of going completely 'mad', a fear of 'disappearing', a fear of going 'outside himself', a fear of 'falling into a bottomless pit'. It is not unusual for a patient to spontaneously link this to a number of specific situations: the fear of an oncoming train and of feeling almost driven to jump under it, a fear of heights such that depth has a frightening but inviting dimension. The next step then leads to claustrophobia and agoraphobia, which contain a common element despite their radically opposite names. Feeling enclosed in a small space is essentially the same as disappearing in a vast expanse.

The man's fear of the woman, and of her presumed desires, is the fear of disappearing into the woman's body. His anxiety is therefore a sexualised form of a much older fear, one that affects both men and women in childhood. Beyond the woman there is the figure of the all-powerful mother, together with a primitive logic. We came from her and therefore the way back is still open.

The sexualised form of this fear hardly exists for the woman—this explains the absence in her of the fear of transgression. However, the fear that does appear in her is the original, general anxiety in an almost unchanged form—the fear of falling, of 'disappearing', of 'going outside herself'. For the little boy and the man, this is translated into a sexualised form—the biting, consuming aspect of sex, the *vagina dentata* of North American Indian mythology. Both presume the same figure: the insatiable mother who desires infinite pleasure and uses her product, her fruit, to this end. The pleasure of the Other is a threat.

The collective rules of the past, which determined the relationship between men and women, have disappeared. Although these rules were formulated for specific places and times, beyond them there was a more fundamental rule that determined and restricted the distribution of pleasure. This too was undermined, and the road to complete pleasure was open. The point has been reached where total enjoyment is almost obligatory, with the only limit a financial one. 'The best of all possible worlds, here! Now!'

The responses to this message of salvation are unexpectedly confusing. Instead of an increase in pleasure, there seems to be a decline of interest in sex, and the long-anticipated disappearance of the restrictive norms has led to a completely new phenomenon. On the one hand, it has resulted in the creation of rules restricted to a single couple, so-called 'mutual consent', which may appear in a contractual form. This is extended to peer groups. Each of these creates new (gender) identities and, in their diversity, they have resulted in the gradual disappearance of the traditional opposition between men and women. On the other hand, there is the conservative reaction of increasing fear and aggression, with the woman as the privileged goal or target; yet the argument is lost. The main reaction of the traditional western man is, above all, flight.

In itself this is not a problem, except for one thing. Despite this existential fear, every 'normal' man is irresistibly driven towards the woman and her presumed pleasure, like a moth to the scorching flame of the candle. He is driven by a drive, and this is our final subject, as well as the most difficult one.

III. The Drive

*'Then I was consumed by the happiness of unification as before
and I fell into a bottomless depth, an experience for which there
are never any words'*
(Hadewijch, *Visions*)

'The horror, the horror'
(*Heart of Darkness, Apocalypse Now*)

Irresistible urges

Mario H., who is 27 years old, has been having a passionate affair with Sylvia D. for three years. One day he discovers that he is sharing the favours of his beloved with
one of his best friends. The relationship changes: there are
tears, threats, quarrels, promises, reconciliation. Mario
believes and doubts, hopes and worries, flung between the
heights of elation and the depths of despair. Again and
again, he looks for signs and discovers reasons for his suspicions—a telephone call that is not answered, unexpected
meetings at work, someone else's hairs in the shower, the
smell of a new perfume. He starts spying on Sylvia's house
and drives round her neighbourhood at night, checking
the parked cars, looking for a light on in her room, searching for reassurance. It is a dubious assurance that he longs
for. Everything that should put his mind at rest is ignored.
The only kind of assurance which convinces him is the
confirmation of his fearful suspicions. One evening when
he sees his friend going into the apartment building, he
feels these suspicions confirmed. He follows him, gets in
with the key (a memory of better times), catches the couple red-handed and kills both of them. When the police
find Mario with the two bodies a few hours later, he keeps

142

saying that he loved Sylvia so much. At his trial, his lawyer talks about an irresistible urge.

This is a strange idea. It implies that there is something happening in us that we cannot resist, something that transcends both reason and the will. A senseless whim is something of mine, yet it takes over from me against my will. The dramatic example of this crime of passion portrays an extreme moment, but the same mechanism is at work whenever the drive manifests itself. The mechanism is as simple as it is frightening. When the drive appears, the conscious, controlling self is taken over. Modern psychology refers to the 'fear of loss of control'. The drive means that one lets oneself go, driven by something else, something coming from an uncontrollable and timeless other place. The field of the drives lies outside consciousness, in a strange but necessary mixture of aggression and Eros.

At first sight, the link with aggression indicates that the drive is above all a male matter. The perpetrators of sexual crimes are almost all men, with women and children in the role of victim. For Freud, the libido was male, a view he based mainly on the fact that this presumed sexual energy always manifested itself in an active and dominating role. From his Victorian perspective, this implied that it must be masculine. It seems that this idea is indeed confirmed by the crime statistics. Women rarely appear in the dock for crimes of sexual passion. When they do, the crime is of an entirely different nature. It is timed, planned and executed in a more conscious way, and the impulsive element is lacking.

This also reveals the direction of the drive—much more from the man to the woman, than the other way round. To conclude from this that the woman is mostly subjected to the drive of the other, and seldom or not at all to her own drives, is to interpret this concept too narrowly. When we

143

look at the purpose of drives later on, we shall have to take this into account. A drive is certainly a driving force. This presupposes a goal, though it is a goal with a paradoxical character, as the person himself is not necessarily happy with it. The question then arises, what or who lies behind this intention?

Crime statistics also show that the perpetrator is virtually always known to the victim. The image of the unknown paedophile waiting in a corner in the dark is a far less frequent reality compared to the sexual violence that occurs in the family, or in a wider context, within the immediate social circle. The step from a man who demands sex from his wife to a man who rapes his partner is often a very small step. This makes the problem of inner division even stronger, culminating in the tender husband who 'in a moment of blind loss of control,' hits his wife, curses her, ties her up, sadistically anally rapes her, and is then taken over by feelings of guilt so that she has to console him.

Trieb, drive, impulse: something drives the subject to a point where he himself does not want to go, where he loses all control. The association with crime makes us forget that every expression of a drive contains an element of violence; a drive without violence is a contradiction in terms. 'Make love not war' is an impossible combination. The drive has an aim that a person is barely aware of, and what can be known about it is often enough for him or her not to want to know any more. 'I don't want to know anything about it'. But he has to know.

When Freud started to develop the foundations of modern psychology, it all looked so simple, in the literal sense that only a single element was involved. The goal built into every person was self-evident—it was the search for pleasure. After all, he argued, everyone avoids unpleasant experiences and unhappiness as much as possible. Surely this goes without saying. Freud's first interpretation of pleasure or happiness still sounds very modern, particularly when it refers to achieving the lowest possible level of tension. Nowadays, we would say little or no negative stress. From this point of view, pain or *un*pleasure is the opposite of pleasure, giving rise to stressful situations that cannot be resolved. These become a source of pain and neurotic symptoms. Freud discovered soon enough that sexuality is the field in which pleasure and unpleasure are experienced most intensely. Unfortunately, the bourgeois morality of his time was very narrow, religious and conservative, and prohibited everything. Children learned very clearly what was allowed and what was forbidden. They took on prohibitions to such an extent that they were restrained on every side. Freud's treatment was intended to liberate them from these external prohibitions and the internal divisions arising from them, so that they could be free to experience pleasure. Psychoanalysis was born as a liberation movement.

A quarter of a century later, an American school of psychology harnessed these very same principles to argue against Freud (the irony of history!) and linked them with a direct pragmatic behavioural therapy. Connecting pleasurable feelings to a particular pattern of behaviour reinforces it, and conversely, negative consequences will eradicate it. Both these theories are based on an undivided person who operates in accordance with a single pleasure principle.

If only it were so simple! At a stroke, education, psychotherapy and criminology would become perfectly operational and predictable practices, and this would be the best of all possible worlds, where pleasure is within everyone's reach. The implicit assumption is that pleasure in this form is the goal that everyone seeks—in fact, the goal of life itself.

A conversation between two little boys aged nine in the back of the car after basketball practice.
- *'Johnny is in love with Anne.'*
- *'Why, how do you know that?'*
- *'Haven't you noticed? He never wants to sit next to her in the car, and when we're training he walks away when she comes anywhere near him. At the New Year's Eve team party he wouldn't even give her a kiss, so he must be in love with her. It's a sure thing.'*

Freud soon discovered that the contrast between individual desire on the one hand, and social and therefore external prohibitions on the other, was not sufficient to explain universal sexual problems. Learned shame, morality and disgust are not an adequate explanation. In 1896, he wrote to his friend Fliess that there must be a source of unpleasure in sexuality itself, which operates independently of society.[1] Pleasure contains an original source of unpleasure and is therefore divided internally in the centre of our being, so that we flee from something in ourselves that drives us where we do not want to go.

The fair comes back every year. Children and adults line up to pay for a ride on brightly coloured fairground attractions that will give them a big dose of tension and fear. The owners of all these colourful rides make use of the same tricks as travelling dentists used a few centuries ago. The event is accompanied by loud music, or what passes for music, to lessen the noise of the shouting and screaming. A little further along, there are posters at the local cinema for the latest horror film. Public executions and tortures in the past were also attended by large numbers of people, and according to Amnesty International, the death penalty does not act as a deterrent, despite all principles of the behaviourists.

The pleasure that is gained from these attractions is very strange, because it borders on pain and torture. The conviction that one is choosing and therefore in control ('I'm paying for it, so I'm making the decision'), combined with the limited length of the ride, means that you remain on the safe side of this border. The thought experiment where the owner decides to extend the ride for an indeterminate length of time transforms the situation into a nightmare, and takes us into the world of Sade, to perversion. Even in this world, agreements are concluded in the form of contracts. We can go (and must go) so far, but no further.

What lies beyond this?

Jekyll and Hyde

In 1886, a Scottish writer who up to that time had not been very successful, had a nightmare from which he awoke screaming. In the six days following this, Robert Louis Stevenson wrote down the story of his dream. The book made history—forty thousand copies were sold within six months—and the title became a proverbial expression in many languages other than English. The book continues to be a best-seller. Since then there has been a good Jekyll and a monstrous Hyde in each of us. The commercial versions continue to appear on screen today—'The Incredible Hulk' is a more recent example.

As a story it follows a certain tradition, and yet it introduces a new element. Up to then, such stories had always made a distinction between two figures, the best known example being the traditional subject of 'Beauty and the Beast'. The ugly, threatening male monster, dangerous and unpredictable, is transformed by the pure and beautiful virgin. The frog—or worse still, the toad, a symbol for all that is disgusting—is transformed by one kiss from the princess into a fairy-tale prince on a white charger, and then there is the knight who must first kill a dragon before winning the hand of a beautiful maiden. These stories never mention the reversible character of this transformation, where the same virgin would see her beautiful prince changing back into a monster.

In Stevenson's version, the division lies in one and the same figure. My copy of the book contains an introduction written in 1955 by a British scholar who made the following comment: 'I am inclined to think that in writing this book Stevenson for the first time completely found himself'. The rest of the paragraph clearly indicates that he meant that Stevenson found himself for the first time as 'a master of words, who developed an English style very much his own, quite unmistakable, full of finesse.' Stevenson certainly did find himself, but not, I suggest, primarily as a writer. The story is echoed in Conrad's *Heart of Darkness* (1902) in which Marlow's search for Kurtz becomes a search for the other half of the seeker himself.

Sixty years later, in the years following the Second World War, the social psychologist Stanley Milgram carried out a number of simple experiments to see how people would react to external pressure (Milgram 1965). Participants in an experiment were asked to administer what they thought were increasingly strong electric shocks to other participants whenever the latter seemed to do anything wrong. The results were frightening—there is a potential torturer in most of us, and it does not take very much for it to reveal itself.

The question is—does this have anything to do with sexuality, with men and women? At first sight it does not seem so. We have reached a 'beyond', lying outside the normal, that is, phallic-genital field of sexuality, a 'beyond' where another field begins. The familiar division is no longer sufficient. Each of us is divided between different desires, between different loyalties to different figures. Men and women are divided, but this is no longer what we are concerned with.

These well-known forms of division conceal another dimension beyond the boundary of what can be expressed in words, where words by definition fail. Perhaps the Stevenson scholar referred to above was right when he defined the author as 'a master of words', since Stevenson was trying to express the ineffable.

What cannot be expressed beyond this boundary is often conceived as a biologically determined heritage—the 'crocodile' in the 'reptile' part of our brain, the point that determines the sort of conduct we do not wish to describe as human. This so-called evolutionary psychology assumes that our brains consist of three parts, roughly corresponding at an evolutionary level to those of reptiles, mammals, and ultimately, via the neo-cortex, to the human being. The older evolutionary parts are presumed to continue to have a 'lower' influence. From this perspective, modern homo sapiens is an incomplete product of evolution, a creature halfway between animal and god, whose imperfections will one day, in another era, be erased and replaced by better characteristics. Meanwhile, we will just have to manage.

This sort of explanation reveals a great deal of ignorance about biology and ethology. So-called inhuman behaviour, often described as 'animal' behaviour, never appears in animals in the natural world and is therefore in fact characteristically human. Reducing drives to an evolutionary atavistic element, to a half-finished product of a blind watchmaker, is just too easy.

So what is it? It is something in the order of a contrast. The drive is the source of a pleasure that is not desired by the subject. Therefore desire and drive are opposites like 'Beauty and the Beast'—or rather, like the familiar 'me' in contrast to the 'not-me'.

It is important to stress here that this 'not-me' nevertheless belongs to myself. The so-called gender conflict ('Beauty and the Beast') is first and foremost an *inner* conflict, of which gender is a handy—but secondary—exteriorisation.

Desire (drive): the never-ending story

The worst thing that can happen to someone who is full of desire is for that desire to be immediately fulfilled. In fact, the word itself conjures up the ideas of delay, longing, something which appears in many poems.

> And my longing cannot move the god of Time:
> But it seems as though the longing owes its name
> To Time, which I want to shorten, and yet long for.
> (P.C. Hooft, *Sonnet*)

To desire is to cultivate a need and enjoy it, in contrast to the immediate gratification of needs as found in animals. This reminds me of the story of the concentration camp prisoner who, when he has been given his meagre rations, waits a while before starting to eat, and in this way remains human. At a less dramatic level, the same phenomenon can be found with so-called luxury articles that all make use of the same principle. The more we pay, the less we get, and the greater the pleasure it gives us. French fries fill us up with calories, while haute cuisine is a sophisticated way of starving us. Need is a relative thing, because anyone who divides his working lunches between The Four Seasons, The Ivy and Chez Nico longs for the forbidden McDonald's round the corner. The Casio watch from the discount store tells us the time and what day it is with an adjustable alarm and chronometer. It is sometimes difficult to tell the time on an expensive Rolex. Cheap porn reveals and gives everything. Erotic literature suggests, postpones, refuses. The lover who carries a letter from his beloved around all day before opening it is unknowingly using the same principle. In short: desire is desire only if it succeeds in postponing something.

In contrast with a drive, desire does not wish to be satisfied in so far as this satisfaction implies an end. On the contrary, assuming that desire has a goal, it is for it to remain intact, to continue. The goal of desire is to go on desiring. *A desire for inconsolability.* The pleasure that is gained from this has a different nature from the pleasure of the fulfilment of this desire. It seems that these are two entirely different pleasures. It is by no means rare for the last form to be experienced as a disappointment, showing that the first type of pleasure was experienced as being more important. A toddler leafing through advertising brochures in the weeks leading up to Christmas is always looking for 'it', trying to make a choice. He/she is actually very little different from the adolescent leafing through forbidden magazines also dreaming of 'it', also hesitating, searching. In each case 'it' can never fulfil the expectation. In the transition from desire to gratification, something is lost that could neither be expressed in the desire nor achieved in its fulfilment.

The essential character of both desire and the time aspect related to it is apparent in the psychopathology that is most closely related to this—depression. The basic complaint of a depressive person can always be reduced to a single sentence, though it appears in two variations: I no longer have any desire, or: no one desires me. The effect of this is that the person feels empty and reduced to nothing. Everything stands still, literally and figuratively. For the depressive patient the dimension of time has been switched off, because time is normally always measured in terms of desire. '. . . X more days to holiday time . . .', 'Next week on Friday, I'll see . . .' Without this, there is no movement, everything becomes catatonic.

The expression 'I've no longer any desire—I'm not desired by anyone' brings us to the most essential dimension of one's own desire: the other person. The goal of the desire may be to continue feeling it, but this goal always has to pass through another person. The idea, sometimes promoted in slogans, of one's *own* desire, quite separate from another person, is an absurdity. A sixteen-year-old pupil, whose marks at school suddenly plummeted, was asked to go and talk to the educational psychologist. The boy said that it was all related to his parents' painful divorce proceedings, which pulled him in often conflicting directions, and he could not cope anymore. The well-meaning psychologist tried to convince him that he was studying not for his parents, but for himself. The next day the boy decided to stop working altogether. After all, he was not doing all this studying just for himself.

Every desire is focused on another person, for or against that person, but never separate from him/her. Independently of the actual content of a desire, it always contains the same implicit question: What am I worth, as a subject of his or her desire, the desire of the other person upon whom mine is focused? This forms the basis for a very typical fantasy that everyone nurtures sooner or later, one that I would call the 'does he/she want to lose me?' fantasy, described in Lacan's work. In the first instance, this sort of daydream shows us our own death—sudden illness, accident, suicide—but focuses above all on the reactions of other people. The other person's feelings of guilt and sorrow that he/she had not been nicer, done more, been different . . . The dreamer sees himself lying in his coffin, attends his own funeral and meanwhile listens to others—*the* other person—missing him.

'*Le désir de l'homme, c'est le désir de l'autre*', a person's desire is the desire for/of another person. This quote is extremely ambiguous. The first meaning, that of a desire 'for the other person' is the most common, and the desire actually increases the more the other becomes unattainable. Just imagine if the two sets of parents of Romeo and Juliet had rented a nice little apartment for them and told them that they really shouldn't take any notice of the family feud but should follow their *own* desire. That would really have been a tragedy! The attraction of the unattainable expresses our ambiguous attitude towards the satisfaction that we are simultaneously seeking.

The other meaning is more difficult—here, the subjective genitive form refers to the desire 'of the other'. Not only do I desire the other person, I also desire the desire *of* that other person, I seek his/her desire for me and want this to be recognised. Within a dual dialectic, this recognition will never be sufficient. After all, a dual relationship or mirror relationship is one in which there can be nothing lacking, so that recognition constantly has to be confirmed. This is caricatured in the couple where the man has to affirm at every meal how delicious everything was. Another variation is the couple where a man always has to know, after making love, whether it was as great for his wife as it was for him. In fact, this sort of relationship is not limited to couples—every interpersonal relationship is subject to this risk. The same applies to the idea of recognition. It always starts from the same point of departure— the desire to be desired by the other—as is clearly expressed, for example, in careers and ambitions for promotion. The advances that are made are disappointing, because by next week there is already another even Bigger Other Person from whom recognition is asked for, demanded and even begged.

The original expression of desire is both sexless and ageless. That which has been described above applies to every couple, heterosexual or gay. Initially it develops in the relationship between other and child, and then rapidly spills over into every other conceivable relationship. The aspect of sex is apparent in the typical complaint which arises from the second meaning—the desire to be desired. Within traditional gender roles, this is expressed as follows. On the part of the woman: 'He doesn't want me, he only wants my body, he's using me'. On the part of the man: 'She doesn't want me, it is always me who takes the first step when we're in bed'. The fact that the very same kind of complaint is fairly well known to homosexual couples proves its general character.

There is an aspect of caricature in this misunderstanding. Both desire the same thing, but both express it in ways that are diametrically opposed. Each desires to be desired by the other person, and each sees rejection in the other

154

person's behaviour. The misunderstanding often goes much further when solutions are contemplated—think of the man, who decides not to initiate making love any more until 'she takes the initiative.' Think of the woman, who decides not to make love any more to 'see whether her husband really wants her, and not just wants her in bed'. It is no coincidence that both belong to one and the same couple, and try out their attempts at a solution at almost the same time.

My desire always goes through the desire of the other person. This means that the field of desire becomes the ultimate field of identification. I identify with the desire I perceive in the other person in order to be desired by him/her. The mirror effects that result from this are not only psychologically abstract but can occur in very concrete forms. In *Metamorphoses*, Ovid writes about Philemon and Baucis. After being a couple all their lives, they start to resemble each other physically. In *Henderson, the Rain King* by Saul Bellow, the king of the Blacks writes a paean to the lion and puts forward a learned argument to the effect that he has started to look like a lion because of his love for and study of this creature. Then Henderson realises that he loves pigs and has always studied them and therefore . . .

Both these examples entail a positive identification and are easily recognisable. In everyday clinical practice, the negative version is found at least as often: a desire aimed *against* the desire of the other person, though with the same goal—to get attention and therefore love. In this way, the subject also has the illusion of having his own desire, clearly distinct from and even going against the desire of the other person.

A couple go to a therapist. He is a lawyer, she is a doctor. The problem is their eighteen-year-old son, a brilliant student but as obstinate as can be. He wants to do his own thing and go to music college to study piano. His parents want him to take up 'serious' study. After all, music is not a real profession. It is at most a pleasant hobby that is useful at family reunions. During the course of three sessions it becomes clear that, as an adolescent, the father had dreamed of becoming an artist and that *his* father had forced him to study law, though he *certainly* does *not* regret that now.

Whose desire are we looking at here? And against whom? Or is it . . . for whom? The conflict between father and son is now seen in quite a different light.

Popular language illustrates this. I am referring here to the expression 'exchanging ideas'. Many couples exchange ideas. They do this as follows. There is a discussion in which the man defends position X, and the woman, position Y. They each put forward their arguments, are convinced they are right and defend their own view. A few days later, the man is in different company and the same discussion occurs. He takes up a position just as enthusiastically putting forward arguments, discussing, and so forth. As he is driving home and thinking about the discussion so that he can tell his wife about it when he gets back, he comes to the astonishing conclusion that, actually, he was defending his wife's position . . .

The 'exchange of ideas' is by no means a rare phenomenon, and is a direct result of the fact that desire works both ways and can therefore result in identification both ways. I identify with her desire (and therefore abandon a previous desire, that is, a previous identification). She identifies with my desire (and consequently also, etc).

Thus the rule is that each of us is divided among different desires based on different identifications: different important other people. This starts at a very early age when we are confronted by the different expectations of our mother and our father. The heartrending question 'Who do you love most, mummy or daddy?' leaves its traces throughout life. Even when the actual question is missing, the sense of being divided still remains and will only increase during the course of development, together with the number of Others.

There is a whole school of psychotherapy based on this structure of desire. Within it, attempts are made to make a distinction between a true self and a false self, between the authentic and the inauthentic part of the personality, between the core of desire and the superficial shell and the like. The aim of the liberating psychotherapy related to this is to be freed from the desire of the other person, with the main aim being learning to say no, choosing for oneself, defending what one really wants for oneself. In practice, this usually amounts to breaking away from the desire of a previous Other, and then aligning oneself with the desire of the next Other. I do not intend to suggest that learning to say no is unimportant. However, the structure of our psyche is such that my desire will always be indebted to that of another, and this is what the choice should be about. Do I make that other person's desire mine or not? Can I bear it if someone appropriates the desire that has been attributed to me, or can't I?

You can exchange ideas about this for ages. I think that you think, that I think, that you think . . . This is the culture of 'talking things through'. Meanwhile, as we are 'talking things through', it is quite possible to make a tacit agreement to avoid what is latently brewing below this desire.

Drive (desire): the immediate

Music by Donizetti, works of art in the background, a young woman is slowly undressing before the camera in an affecting but amateurish way. A middle-aged man is looking on, staring at her without moving. When the woman drops the last article of clothing, he leaves abruptly—'it' is all over. The drive has been satisfied, the man can go on his way—until the next time.

This 'it' cannot be named. The rest of the film—*Man of Flowers*, by Paul Cox—makes us experience what 'it' is about. The drive is revealed all the more clearly because, for once, it is not the cheap sensation-seeking expression of the drive that is shown, but the drive that forms the very basis of the medium of film itself, namely wanting to see or be seen. Exhibitionism and voyeurism are well-known but poorly understood phenomena. The film takes us back to childhood via flashbacks, showing a mother whose mouth reveals both sensuality and rejection, and a child who wants to see and feel, and is both attracted and rejected. Once he is an adult, he takes control—he pays the young woman generously—always looking for what he could not find in his mother either.

The contrast between drive and desire is not what we might expect here, particularly the contrast between Beauty and the Beast, what is 'noble' and what is 'animal'. The contrast lies primarily between what is familiar to the subject and what is strange to him, what the subject knows and recognises in himself, and what he refuses and places outside himself. The whole scenario serves to keep the two worlds separate. The subject of the desire does not recognise himself in the subject of the drive. It is 'outside him'. In the rest of the film the young woman falls in love with the man. In fact, she falls in love with his fascination for her, which she feels in his gaze. She falls in love with herself in the mirror of his eyes. On the basis of this desire she begins to talk, something she has not done before. She even offers herself (*'Do you want me to stay with you tonight?'*). The result is that she breaks the mirror, she enters his world, his familiar world, and therefore has to leave the other world. When she asks him why he no longer plays Donizetti, and barely looks up when she performs her act, he says: *'I started to talk to you'*.

The immediacy of the drive contrasts with the continuity of desire. This contrast not only relates to the aspect of time, but goes much further. Desire is mediated in the sense that the figuration of the desired object is central, so that desire is the theme of all artistic expression, that is, of all representation. Earlier I noted that one of the most central elements of eroticism is not so much crude gratification as its representation, its expression through the imagination. This is contrasted with the drive as an unmediated phenomenon, impossible to represent, seeking a psychological anchor but stumbling in a short circuit of a single moment followed by another attempt, and thus falling into a constant repetition.

Freud summarised this in his account of the drive as a borderline concept situated between the body and the mind, thus characterising it as a typically human phenomenon that could never appear in animals. There is something—he refers to a pressure and a source—that arises from the body or rather from the outer limits of the body. All the so-called erogenous zones are transitions between the inside and the outside: the mouth, penis/vagina, nipple, anus, but also the nose, eye, ear and skin. What rises up is something like energy, looking for a way out and a discharge through an object and an associated aim. The drive is related to this impossible transition between the two. Indeed, the drive *is itself* this impossible transition between the source and the pressure on the one hand, and the aim and the object on the other.

This explains the rest of Freud's description. The drive is a measure of the work demanded of the psyche as a result of its connection with the body. The man of flowers in the film is constantly looking for, but cannot find 'it', because 'it' disappears in the transition from one medium, the body, to the other, the spirit. He starts to collect beauty in the vain hope that a collection of art can provide an answer to something that cannot be represented. Just as easily, this could go the other way, the drive leading to the drivenness of passion. 'It' doesn't work, and this leads to a fury that must go somewhere. Caresses turn to blows and the collection is smashed.

Usually the drive is reduced to this latter activity, and it is thought that this impulse is a biological part of the human being, the 'reptile brain' discussed above. This sort of reduction reveals a total lack of understanding of ethology and always omits something that actually forms the essence of the drive. The message it sends is simple to refute. The message is as follows: everything I do wrong is a result of the animal in me (and therefore, as a human, I have nothing to do with it). The poison of the snake, the greed of the wolf, the cowardice of the hyena, the cruelty of the crocodile, the obscenity of the monkey . . . Whenever a human being regresses to these so-called primitive drives, it is supposedly the animal element that emerges.

I submit that it is exactly at these moments that he is farthest removed from the natural, biological state. Animals have no Auschwitz, no Kosovo. The element of biology cannot turn into psychology and, conversely, the element of psychology cannot become biology. The drive appears in the no-man's-land between these two and is the effect of this impossible crossing of the borders. The anger and aggression that often accompany it are always expressions of impotence and helplessness that are unknown to animals. Animals have instincts, not drives.

The source and the pressure can never acquire a suitable form of expression in the psyche, that is a representation and a name that would make them controllable by the subject. This is structurally impossible because, from the moment that it is given a name, the drive is no longer a drive but belongs to a different order, that of reflectivity, of distancing and mediation. A boundary has been crossed, and what has been taken from one side to the other seems not so much to have disappeared, as to have been transformed once it has reached the other side.

Transgressions of the drive confront us with an intuitive understanding. The drive begins wordlessly, or at most with cries and meaningless screams. The border is reached when screaming turns to swearing and violent expletives. A moment later the line is crossed and there is speech. Subjectivity, reflection and distancing begin and the drive is transformed. Anyone at risk of being raped must get the rapist to speak.

It is also possible to cross the border from the other side. Words start to fail, the subject disappears and makes way for an uncontrollable flow of energy that sweeps away any distance and mediation and results in a being-there, solid and fluid at the same time. It is a dizzying experience on the roller coaster that releases all the vital juices; it is the ecstasy of disappearing in the screaming crowd; it is the overwhelming panic attack in which we lose 'ourselves'. It is the eternity between the beginning of the orgasm in which the 'self' seems to disappear completely, and the last paroxysm in which subjectivity returns with great intensity.

This is what is known as jouissance, the energy of plea-sure linked to the drive that has taken over the reins and leaves the desiring subject behind. This abandonment is necessary because without it, one becomes a sort of 'observer', seeing oneself being active and constantly eval-uating oneself ('Am I doing this right?'). It is like someone who is travelling and who, during the trip itself, is already preparing the story that he will tell his friends when he returns home.

Leaving ourselves behind is the precondition for jouis-sance. The question is then—who or what enjoys the plea-sure here? It is the rule rather than the exception that for the ego, the very first appearance of this jouissance is noth-ing more than anxiety, the harbinger of one's own disap-pearance. I disappear, and being takes over. No wonder that jouissance is what the ego does not want. The price is ceasing to exist as an ego. The fact that this anxiety is trans-formed into ecstasy does not reduce the price to be paid. In this light, desire should be seen as a defence against the drive and jouissance. A defence against something that gives one pleasure, though the status of the word 'one' is not quite clear in this context, and the concept of 'pleasure' is also strange.

The ego's fear of jouissance can be understood in terms of the experience of time that is linked to it, and therefore in terms of the distinction between desire and drive. Desire is measured in terms of time, with commas, semi-colons, question marks, exclamation marks and full stops. This kind of delineation provides an anchor, and therefore security. These are lacking in jouissance, so there is a risk that the ego will be lost, disappear in its boundlessness, never to return. In the 'usual' expression of the drive—the sexual act in the narrow coital meaning of the term—the body has a built-in safety mechanism with a direction and end point, namely, the genital orgasm. The boundaries are defined and the energy is channelled. The aim is a climax: the dam breaks, but the goal is in sight. The cry, 'I'm coming, I'm coming' is wholly appropriate, because until then this 'I' was nowhere to be found. This safe form of jouissance is the phallic, orgasmic form that stops at a prescribed station. It is well known that the man, in particular, needs this sort of final point though the reason for this is still unclear. I shall say more about this in what follows.

What happens if there is no such final point? Imagine a man or woman constantly brought to ecstasy at ever higher, ever increasing levels, the roller coaster that keeps on going round, the screaming crowd that cannot be calmed down. Every mass revolution ends in a paroxysm of blood, in comparison with which soccer hooliganism is child's play.

The drive is inherently traumatic.

Drive and trauma

At the end of the nineteenth century, Freud frequently came to the conclusion that his patients, usually female, had been the victims of sexual abuse. The fact that the perpetrator belonged to the immediate family and was often the father could not be publicised at that time. As a result, there were rather a lot of perverted 'uncles' described in scientific articles. The consequences of this sort of abuse for the victims were very complex, because they affected both the body and the mind and had a very specific influence on the way in which patients related to other people. It was by no means rare for there to be an attitude of sexual provocation, and the phenomenon was initially known as 'conversion hysteria'. Treatment was long and difficult.

Ten years later, Freud revised his theory. The universal occurrence of hysteria in Victorian Vienna would have meant that the population could be roughly divided into two halves: the perverted abusers and the abused hysterics. He reworked his theory with a clear shift of emphasis. He no longer considered that sexual abuse was the cause, or the sole cause, but also investigated the fantasies that the patient had constructed with the purpose of assimilating a trauma that might or might not have occurred in reality. Psychological disturbances had to be understood and studied mainly in terms of these fantasies. After all, it was this fantasy world that would determine the patient's reality. 'All the world's a stage.' Every player is given his role and plays his part, and we ourselves diligently help to write the script.

Little Clara had to go to the dentist. Her older brother—already ten years old, and therefore a figure of some authority—has really terrified her. There is the injection, the drill, the noise. The expected pain is experienced, but Clara is brave and (figuratively) grits her teeth. When she comes home she plays the same game with her dolls for weeks on end: playing dentists, and *she* is the dentist.

This example shows the function of the imagination—rewriting a scenario so that one has a better role than before, and the buck can be passed on. 'Better' usually means active and controlling, instead of passive and subordinate. The step to carrying out such a fantasy in reality is very small, and has the effect that each of us is the director of our own world, giving out 'roles' and choosing 'actors'. Our reality has the structure of fiction.

Jane R. is 32 years old. Her parents separated when she was four, and both remarried shortly afterwards. When she was seven, an uncle on her mother's side started to play sex games with her. When she was twelve, she was raped by her stepfather with threats of violence. From then on, he regularly used her sexually. Her mother didn't notice anything and treated her as a sort of Cinderella figure. When she was sixteen, she took an overdose of her mother's tranquillisers and received psychiatric treatment for the first time. She told 'everything', and after staying for a few months she went back home, though this time she went to her father's new family. After a few months her brother started to abuse her sexually, and once again she fell into the Cinderella role with her stepmother. More than ten years later, after all sorts of referrals to psychiatric services, and with a history of self-mutilation and drug addiction, she moved into a supervised home. Within six months a sadomasochistic relationship developed between Jane and one of the female housing officers, and this required medical treatment of the genitalia. A year later she was pregnant—the probable father was one of the psychotherapists. Jane was described as a provocative borderline case, with paranoid tendencies, who repeatedly succeeded in misleading others. While originally she was given credit because of her role as a victim, she was now rejected as a schemer.

Whose drive, whose trauma are we talking about? The naïve distinction made between the victim and the perpetrator ignores the complexity of these situations. Building up an initially fantasised strategy for survival results in unexpected role reversals that imperceptibly turn into reality. The victim *does* become a victim again, but she or he has helped to set the scene, so that the apparently passive position is deceptive and conceals an actively organising position in control of the situation. It makes the tragedy of the victim all the greater.

This kind of self-destructive scenario for the victims of long-term sexual abuse is by no means unusual, and forms a long drawn-out psychological version of something that also appears in a shorter, purely physical way—self-mutilation. To the outsider, this symptom is completely incomprehensible—these victims have already suffered so much that their bodies bear the traces, and then they go on to injure themselves, to cut, slash, burn. The well-meaning helper is unwittingly put in the role of a carer-guard, and before you know where you are, there is yet another power struggle, a game of cat and mouse in which it is not at all clear who is the cat and who is the mouse.

Self-mutilation of this kind has a very distinctive character. In contrast to the provocative, hysterical version,[2] where someone threatens to injure themselves in the presence of an audience, and thus tries to attract attention ('Do you want to lose me?'), the traumatic version of self-mutilation takes place in secret, in the privacy of the patient's relationship with his/her own body. When these patients talk about it, they give the impression that they are trying to describe something that cannot be expressed in words, either at the moment at which they act, or afterwards, and that the self-mutilation was the only remaining possibility. They describe a condition of physical tension that suddenly erupts and spirals up until it becomes a maelstrom in which the ego becomes liquid, empties, and disappears, so that the body is at risk of bursting out of its seams, subjected to an indescribable experience—and the next moment the last remnant of the ego cuts into the body until the blood flows. The tension disappears, calmness returns and there is a sense of relief in the victim, of 'being back'. There is a cloud of guilt and shame about this act, as though something unhealthy has happened, and it is therefore hidden from the outside world.

It does not take much imagination to recognise the drive in this description, though it is literally a misplaced drive, an unlocalised drive that spreads through the whole body without being able to turn on the usual escape valve, so that jouissance increases to the point where, in utter despair, an emergency exit has to be cut out. Self-mutilation is a form of auto-eroticism.

The comparison with 'ordinary' masturbation reveals similarities and differences. A woman who is driven by an inner accumulation of tension and seeks an orgasmic release, if necessary reaching a climax against the corner of a table, knows the same tension and release as the traumatised patient who resorts to self-mutilation. The difference is that, in the latter, the focus of the physical release through the genital channel is lacking, and another outlet must be created. As incomprehensible as this may seem, it can be clinically demonstrated. As a phenomenon, it is reminiscent of another curious fact found in the clinical treatment of patients suffering from the traumatic war neurosis. A soldier who is exposed to bombing for hours and is then injured on top of it all, will probably escape developing a traumatic neurosis. It clearly does not make much difference what causes the blood to flow, self-mutilation or mutilation by others, as long as it flows. The distinction between the subject and the other becomes incomprehensibly vague at this point and requires further examination.

Descriptions of self-mutilation and of sexual abuse reveal a common characteristic. In both cases, the victim describes something that comes *from outside*, and that he or she is powerless to resist. In the case of sexual abuse, this is quite clear; it is another person's drive that has the traumatic effect. The step we can take from here to self-mutilation is that a person's *own* drive can be experienced as being just as strange, frightening and even traumatic. The victims of so-called traumatic neurosis manifest in an exaggerated and distorted way what is present in a 'normal' person: we all have to come and go with our drive.

On the basis of this reasoning, everyone seems to suffer from a structurally determined traumatic neurosis. From a very early age we are all subject to drives that cry out for fulfilment, answers, a form. Everyone will remember the drivenness behind playing 'doctors and nurses', the search for what cannot be spoken, wanting to know, the passion of the little child that is no less intense than that of the adult. An adult who thinks this can be resolved with appropriate sex education will find it largely ineffective. Pure biology is pale by comparison with wanting to know what is really going on. The child builds up his or her own knowledge partly on the basis of what is heard and partly on the basis of what is experienced in his or her own body, knowledge that then leads to further experiences. There is a constant friction between the two—the confrontation between what is expected and what actually happens is always out of balance. There is either too little or too much, it is too early or too late. A meeting that is always missed, so that the movement of the wheel known as life continues to turn.

Drive drives the subject beyond his own boundaries. As long as it is merely a matter of desire, life is a bed of roses, there is laughter and tears and, above all, talk. This is the safe side of the road! Beyond a desire for another person, I am both attracted and repelled by jouissance— can I allow myself to be the passive object of pleasure, can I become active in relation to this jouissance? It is no longer even clear whose pleasure is involved, whether it is my own or that of another. This very vagueness, this lack of words, is a source of attractiveness. All someone has to do is be considered a mysterious, or even a dangerous source of pleasure and he/she at once becomes the centre of attraction toward whom everything flows, or conversely, from whom everything flees. It is a typical characteristic of jealousy and hatred to envy another person for his or her presumed pleasure. The main message of the Nazi propaganda against the Jews emphasised their jouissance at the expense of Aryans. A majority of the mocking caricatures showed dirty little men rubbing their hands in glee, faces dripping with repellent pleasure, warnings against the dangers of consorting with them, and the like. The fact that this was at the same time a direct advertisement was not yet appreciated by the propaganda psychologists of that era. Now they know better. A pervert is always described as someone who has access to a very attractive, but very dangerous jouissance. Even in westerns we feel attracted to the baddies, the men in black.

The presumed pleasure of the other person is at my expense—will I go along with this, or won't I? Traditionally this question is seen to apply within the interpersonal relationship, but it should primarily be understood *internally*. The jouissance of the drive, that other dimension at work in me, takes place at the expense of me as a subject—will I go along with this or won't I? The answer to this internal question will determine the answer to the external relationship.

The first reaction is predictable: defence.

The forbidden apple

There is something curious about desire. I inevitably yearn for something that is forbidden to me, inaccessible, unhealthy. But above all, forbidden. Experience has certainly shown that everything that gives pleasure is either unhealthy or immoral. As my daughter once said when she was five, 'Healthy, but still nice!' The mature realisation that the grass that looks greener on the other side looks greener only when seen from my side, does not change this very much, except that it highlights the dimension of forbidden fruit and the other side even more strongly. It is not what or who is on the other side, but the fact that it is on the other side. The traditionally forbidden apple gives more pleasure than the apple that is permitted, and, at the same time, this additional pleasure results in a feeling of guilt. The next step is to cultivate this dimension for itself. Once upon a time this resulted in something like the courtly lover, the relationship between the troubadour who pledged himself to 'his' lady and serenaded her, but remained at a distance. In Japanese culture there were geishas on whom the samurai lavished fortunes in order to spend just one chaste evening with them.

These Japanese samurai were not Catholics. Though this may sound banal, it means that a popular view must be questioned, namely, that the link between desire and prohibition is only a result of the extremely strict Catholic-Protestant ethic of the last centuries. It is tempting to adopt this sort of view as an explanation because it is so simple and particularly because the remedy is clear: free yourself from the external oppressor! This idea will always be successful—it is enough to say the word for everyone to nod their agreement. Academic freedom, the freedom of the press, freedom of religion, poetic freedom thus become arguments that are not to be questioned further, and that will settle a discussion and silence opponents.

As far as I know, Michel Foucault is one of the few who does not fall into this trap. The second part of *The History of Sexuality* is devoted to Greece in the classical period and starts by describing traditional expectations that boil down to western European idealisation of what we expect of the Greek grass on the other side: the absence of compulsory monogamy, a positive view of the sexual act and the idealisation of love between men and boys. It surprises us when he then states that these expectations are wrong. In fact, he claims, the roots of the Catholic ethic are actually to be found in this Greek way of thinking. He then goes on to study these roots beyond mere facile slogans, in a style and language that are not intended for the impatient modern reader.

A study of a non-Catholic culture can be seen as a kind of scientific experiment in which one examines how a particular hypothesis turns out if one omits a component that has been assumed to be essential. Greek culture from the fourth century certainly exhibits striking differences from our own. In the first place, our expression 'sexuality' did not exist at all. As both Foucault and Van Ussel have shown, this term was introduced only at the end of the nineteenth century. This is important, if only because it shows that what we mean by sexuality is not an unchanging concept, but simply a historically bound phenomenon. Consequently, Foucault did not talk about the sexuality of the Greeks, but about *the use of pleasure*,[3] which covers three subjects—eating, drinking and eroticism. In other words, the relationship of pleasure that I adopt towards the intimate stranger, that is, in the first instance, *my own body*, and in the second instance, that of another.

His study shows that this relationship was the basis of a project for a very typical form of ethical self-care. Classical Greek culture developed a male morality that invited the free citizen to participate in what Foucault called self-practices, in contrast to the later Catholic system of externally imposed rules. The central element of this morality is the emphasis on austerity, with *enkrateia* and *sophrosyne* as the main themes. *Enkrateia* is the attitude of self-mastery that one must adopt in order to function as a moral subject. *Sophrosyne* is the related combination of moderation and wisdom. Together this results in an image of 'true' freedom, which is not the paradox it may seem because what is meant is freedom from *inner* slavery, through the achievement of a condition of total self-sufficiency and perfect sovereignty over oneself. This is where the concept of truth comes in, truth in the sense of self-knowledge. *Gnothi seauton*, know thyself.

From our perspective, this means that the dimension of prohibition certainly does apply, but by different means. In the first place, it is mainly aimed at drives, and much less at desire. Further, for the Greeks of the classical period, with the exception of incest there was virtually no prohibition on any specific sexual practices. Their morality was concerned not with the nature, but rather with the quantity and intensity of the use of pleasure, with the aim of rationing it. A man who surrendered wholly to food, drink and sex was considered a weakling. A closer examination of this need for rationing produces an unexpected result. For the Greeks such an attitude was reprehensible, *because it amounted to adopting the passive position*. It focused on the man who submitted passively, either to his own body or to that of another, and *that* was seen as the ultimate evil. Therefore the Greek attitude can be interpreted as a cultivation of the active, dominating approach.

Subsequently, Catholic morality made two important changes. Authority was imposed externally by God and the Church on pain of punishment, and, at the same time, the content of what was forbidden was defined. The Church fathers not only demanded moderation to the point of complete abstinence, but in addition, an ever-increasing number of sexual activities were both described and proscribed. In this way, Catholicism shifted the emphasis from drives to desires. All this was directed from outside by God the Father to whom absolute obeisance was due. There was not even freedom of thought, because merely thinking, imagining or contemplating punishable acts was considered a sin.

This change is particularly important, because it externalises what was formerly an internal relation and internal division, and subjects it to an external authority. It was the Church that established the Name-of-the-Father.

Thus Greece taught the moderation of the drive—Catholic Rome forbade even desire. The hyperbolic development of this prohibition gave rise to the frustrated middle classes who came knocking at Freud's door at the end of the nineteenth century. When he took the first steps towards explaining neurosis and sexuality, he was confronted with the divisions inherent in the subject. Everyone is divided between what they desire and what they fear. The explanation for this was thought to be obvious. Exaggeratedly strict social rules inevitably had to result in neurosis and a double morality. The gradual psychotherapeutic working-through of this anxiety, the gratifying liberation of the patient from this strict morality, was not without effects, but the anticipated results failed to materialise. Beyond Rome, Athens is waiting.

However, neurosis cannot be fully explained by the contrast between an individual's desires and social prohibitions. These prohibitions certainly do exist, and in 1900 were even abundant, but it is not enough merely to remove them. The error in reasoning here is that these prescriptions and proscriptions are thought to be the *cause*, the cause of frustration and tension in the individual. Dealing with them through therapy shows that they are also the *result*, the result of an internal need for regulation in the subject him/herself, to which they are a response. The fact that the style of this response far exceeded its goal at the time is a historical detail that has now been corrected. Meanwhile, the contemporary correction is also in danger of exceeding its aim, and consequently the internal need for control is becoming ever clearer. The limits have been reached and the search for new boundaries is in full swing.

Freud's theory can also be read as a single protracted attempt to understand this internal need for control, in other words, the way in which human beings try to cope with the drive. For example, he describes obsessional neurosis as a defence against a surfeit of pleasure, and hysteria as a defence against a surfeit of unpleasure. From the beginning, there was a link with trauma, and initially his argument was couched in terms of the traditional roles of the sexes at the time. The male obsessional neurotic fled from the active, grasping nature of his own drives, while the female hysteric fled from being passively taken over by the drives of another. However, these positions are reversible, and the interpretations of 'male' and 'female' are increasingly relative terms in his ideas, to be interpreted as two poles in a single individual. Certainly, I am *not* referring to a kind of primordial bisexualism in the human being. On the contrary, these two poles *precede* any form of gender. The only remaining interpretation is that of the contrast between a passive and an active attitude, and the way in which a subject chooses a position with respect to these. Such a choice is made in the field of desire, and thus both in relation to another person and in relation to the otherness of one's own body, whether it is a male or a female body. Beyond all the various ways of dealing with it (narcissism, projection, identification, repression, sublimation, etc), one central point remains which clearly must be dealt with—the need for defence.

Freud completed his career with an account of what underlies defence, what arouses the greatest anxiety and therefore requires the most treatment. He chivalrously admitted that even lengthy analysis could not provide any cure for this and that analysis at this level became *'unendlich'* (interminable). Furthermore, he discovered that what must be addressed is the same for men and women, that it is, at most, the external manifestations that differ. Everyone flees from a passive position in relation to the Other; what everyone must deal with is the anxiety that this arouses.

Athens and Vienna have become brothers.

What Freud did not recognise is that what is most avoided is also most desired. Beyond anxiety there is a desire for this passive position, for being submitting to the other person, the other thing. To disappear in it.

Transgression: the sado-masochistic universe

Sadism and masochism are weak terms, and meaningless because they are derived from proper nouns and are therefore open to all sorts of vague interpretations. Erotic trade fairs market all sorts of whips, shackles and collars, but when he or she goes home, the purchaser doesn't really know what to do with them. The spark that was ignited is now extinguished.

One long-lost childhood pastime was playing cowboys and indians, when the red-skins were the bad guys and the white man was the good guy—very politically incorrect. Usually, the girls were made to play indians, while the boys preferred to be the cowboys and would only change roles if the girls really insisted. After all sorts of wild chases, trying to grab others, the first part of the game would end in triumphantly tying up the captured red-skins to the totem pole. We had learned our knots with the boy scouts. The second part of the game consisted in all sorts of tortures that nearly managed to scare the life out of the prisoners, mainly by telling them about all the things that could happen. I remember one extremely inventive cowgirl—she would never agree to be an Indian—who had these tortures 'carried out' by an intermediary, her favourite doll. It was always placed on the head of the tied-up victim, the screaming red-skin, and it was then told to pee. The fact that this was actually a real possibility with the technically advanced doll increased the hilarity even further.

The cowgirl is now a poet—not a bad one either.

The adult version of this game produces the same pleasure. It is agreed that one person will adopt the oppressed, humiliated, immobilised position and surrender to the arbitrary behaviour of the dominating other, who issues orders, curses, threatens to do 'it', and even makes advances. The victim screams, begs, prays, … and enjoys. It looks exactly like a nightmare in which we are surrendering to something that drives us to the edge, to the point where 'it' will happen: the monster that will jump on us, the fall into the depths, being grabbed—but just before this we wake up, screaming with fear. Saved by the bell.

For Freud, the nightmare is the only exception to his general view that every dream contains a wish fulfilment. His correction is wrong. The nightmare is the ultimate—and therefore impossible—wish fulfilment that tries to take gratification to the point of no return. The question is: wish fulfilment for whom or what? We haven't got there yet.

The three situations—children's games, adult scenarios and nightmares—all have more or less the same structure, a passive subordination to the pleasure of the grasping other. The difference lies in the way in which limits are imposed. Both in children's and in adults' games, the limits are agreed on. Everyone takes turns being an Indian. When the victim has had enough, you can go on for just a moment, but only just a moment; violations are punished: 'you can't play anymore'. In a nightmare, there is a sort of automatic ejection chair that catapults the subject back into his everyday existence.

These boundaries are absolutely essential. When they are absent, the real daytime nightmare starts, in the form of perversion or psychosis. Jouissance is possible only when the boundaries have been put into place to create a limit. In accordance with the dual nature of the drive, this limit can function at two levels. There is an as yet incomprehensible physical level: orgasm, automatically waking up during a nightmare, self-mutilation. The common characteristic of these three somatic safety valves is the return of the active ego, coupled with a mixture of relief and disappointment. The limit can also be imposed at the collective, psychological level: agreement, rules establishing the limits in advance on the basis of a convention and an assurance that they will be observed. There may even be a collective agreement to suspend the rules for a limited period and within a limited area. Every culture, particularly the strictest and most disciplined, has a carnival, a feast of the flesh in which anything and everything is possible, any transgression of the bounds of everyday rationality, within defined limits of time and space.

The scene: Thebes, in front of the palace. The event: Agave staggers into the square in ecstasy, triumphantly carrying a severed head in her bloodied hands. She cheers and sings: under the influence of Bacchus she has caught a wild animal together with her sisters, not with nets, not with spears, but with her bare hands. Together they drove it into a corner and tore it to pieces with their nails and teeth, screaming and howling; now she comes to show off her booty.

The head is that of Pentheus, her own son.

The story is that of Euripides' tragedy *The Bacchae*, and the scene is one of the most gruesome from the plays that have come down to us. As a story, it is the counterpart to Orestes, with Oedipus as the middle point between the other two. Orestes escapes from the mother, Oedipus just fails to escape, Pentheus loses all the way.

The tragedy is based on a tradition full of mystery, in which reality is difficult to establish. Bacchus is the god of wine and sensuality. He is, above all, the dying god constantly being reborn; his Egyptian predecessor is Osiris. The rituals devoted to him are those of the women known as the Bacchantes or maenads. Secret rites take place in the forests on the mountain slopes, and are strictly forbidden to men. The women are brought into a state of ecstasy by song, dance, drink, and also by mushrooms (according to Robert Graves, *amanita muscaria*) around a living incarnation of Bacchus, usually a male goat. At the climax of the ritual, they throw themselves onto the animal, tear it to pieces with their bare hands and devour the quivering bits of raw meat. At this point they literally become 'enthusiastic' which in Greek means that they have taken up God into themselves. Traditionally, every man in the area, any passer-by or deliberate spy, will undergo the same fate.

Pentheus wished to see the women and had therefore disguised himself as a woman.

In the West, there are some scattered remnants of this story, in both a profane and a sacred version. The profane version is the witches' sabbath, where vixens were believed to dance around the fire, devouring children and having intercourse with the Devil. The sacred version involves 'the body of Christ', and communion as a ritual meal represents being assimilated into the wider community of this other dying God the Son, who also constantly rises from the dead. The element of 'enthusiasm' for incorporating the god, has been considerably reduced, and Catholics barely realise now that they are participating in a totem meal. You are what you eat.

Enthusiasm: being full of the Other, quite literally in the case of the Bacchantes. Enthusiastically being full and being fulfilled is directly opposed to the emptiness of depression and the sense of abandonment by the Other. While at the level of desire we can still be satisfied with identification, assimilating the desire of the other, the drive goes much further. It goes further back. It now becomes the incorporation, the literal assimilation of the Other, a long way past the timid kiss. Oral sex is a weak remnant in which the effect of power can occasionally be glimpsed. A recent survey showed that many women experience fellatio as a sense of power—on condition that they take the initiative, and that it is not imposed on them, in other words, on condition that they take the active role.

Enthusiasm is accompanied by a strange phenomenon, strange in comparison with its original meaning of 'full of the Other'. I mean: *ecstasy*. Literally, ecstasy means 'standing outside yourself'. It is not only Pentheus who disappears, the maenads also disappear, Bacchus disappears, and together they dissolve into a nameless symbiosis far beyond their individual egos. It is no coincidence that orgiastic rites and orgies are group events. Having an orgy on your own hardly ever works out. The essence of an orgy is the disappearance of the individual into a greater whole, in a group that has replaced the normal rules by other ones. The limitations of genital orgasm are replaced by the ecstatic enthusiasm of the group, a curious kind of total jouissance that interconnects the individuals and therefore erases them. This is the same experience that may occur with certain gatherings of religious sects. I heard the most insightful description from a former member of such a sect. She described it as an orgasmic experience, but a hundred times more powerful than the ordinary sexual climax, and linked to something that she described as 'speaking in tongues', the moment at which the body starts to speak 'of its own accord', though in an unintelligible language. This is the moment at which jouissance spills over. It was only later, when she had left the sect, that the experience became frightening. This link with religion has been present since time immemorial. The Bacchanalia were religious feasts, 'mysteries', in which the unintelligible aspects of life and death were celebrated in a frenzied manner.

Euripides' tragedy illustrates the ultimate point of the sadomasochistic universe, the outermost limit of transgression, in which sexuality is no longer confined to its genital-phallic aspect but continues the return to the very first oral relationship, literally devouring love. The link with anxiety and aggression is all the more clear as a result. This link was forged quite early in the history of psychoanalysis. Psychopathological disorders resulting from sexual trauma are very similar to trauma caused by war. They can both be interpreted as the effects of unbridled violence with an almost complete absence of the normal rules. In a recent study by Judith Herman, the two groups, patients traumatised by sex or by war, were studied side by side without too many questions about the parallels. The expression 'an orgy of violence' connects the two. Here too, the group character remains essential.

The study of war neurosis is extremely interesting. Its involuntary nature results in a gruesome group experiment that can be used to clarify a number of matters. The study of the Vietnam War was particularly instructive in this context. Surrendering to violence is facilitated by being part of a group, and has little traumatic effect as long as the group association remains very strong. It is the fighting unit as a collectivity that makes transgression possible, in a way that goes much further than any form of imagining. In fact, it is precisely the failure of imagination that facilitates action. 'Go, go, go!' If and when the group disintegrates, trauma can arise, and in the case of the Vietnam soldiers it often occurred after their always individual—and therefore isolated—return from their tour of duty. Separated from the group and the rules of the group, they were confronted with what retrospectively became traumatic. In popular terminology, they were 'haunted by images and memories.' But this expression is not correct— the veterans were actually haunted by the *impossibility* of expressing 'it' in words and images. It was the unimaginable that continued to persecute them in a real way. A traumatised person does not remember the trauma, but experiences it over and over again.

What happened later is, if anything, even more interesting. In the absence of any official attention and care, the Vietnam War could not be discussed for a whole generation, and the veterans united in self-help groups. These groups, usually composed of African-Americans, actively started to work on their traumatic past together. From this there arose their own culture, their own symbolic representations, which led to an attempt to cope with the trauma through symbolising and expressing their traumatic experiences. The result is now widely known as rap music.

The drive lies on the boundary between the body and the mind, between immediate wordlessness and its representation, the element that cannot or can hardly be expressed, and that operates in a shadow zone. Rap is, in its origin, a primitive primal attempt at mastery through a first step towards symbolisation. The primitive element lies in the choice of the rhythm, subordinating unprocessed pieces of jouissance to rhythmic shouting in a group, for the group, by the group, thus actively creating an ecstatic enthusiasm, one that, moreover, allows for a return of the ego. It is precisely because this active rhythm breaks through the timeless, unmediated aspect of jouissance and announces the return of the self, that it is so effective.

For me, rap is reminiscent of the head banging of a child who cannot fall asleep and tries to overcome its fear of the dark and the yawning hole of the window. It is also reminiscent of incantatory rituals as described by historical anthropology, the prayers and chants with which the shamans try to understand the incomprehensible aspect of the body, and thus to take hold of it and control it. Lévi-Strauss showed the far-reaching effect of this in his paper, 'L'efficacité symbolique'. Shakespeare was also familiar with this phenomenon. The witches in *Macbeth* are really rap artists and it is no coincidence that they dance round the cauldron ('Double, double, toil and trouble—fire burn, and cauldron bubble'). Anyone who has seen a performance by a group of Japanese Kodo drummers has also experienced the physical power of rhythm.

The meaning of these experiences appears only later. The rhythm is of primary importance. It is the same rhythm that underlies any form of martial music, the drum-rolls, marching music, tom-toms, the piercing shrieks of Muslim women urging on the warriors. It is a way of dealing with fear prior to the ecstasy, with a characteristic insensitivity to pain—there is no ego left to feel pain. The same rhythmic path can be used to return, for the rebirth of the ego. With rap, the Vietnam groups—peer groups, that is to say, fatherless groups—intuitively discovered this way of working through their trauma. The comparison with previous musical currents reveals changes from the past to the present: what rap does for jouissance, the blues did for desire. Desire relates to the individual, the intensified sense of self that sings out its impotence, and therefore its shortcomings, in long drawn-out tones. Jazz anticipates the drive and requires more processing. Rap is an attempt at dealing with the excess.

On the fringe of this collective processing, the members developed a group identity. It is not surprising that they were popularly known as 'the brothers'. Consequently every member could distil his own identity, his own ego, from this group. Group identity essentially means rules, and therefore security. Every group is concerned with regulating jouissance.

With a little help from my friends . . .

Post-modern musical styles are indicative of the contemporary surfeit of pleasure. The 'no-rules' generation does not know what to do with this surfeit and resorts to the most primitive, in the sense of primordial attempts to deal with it. Thus piercing as a new style is no more than ritualised self-mutilation, with the same function as 'ordinary' mutilation. It has taken over from tattoos, which at least still had the character of representation, albeit inscribed on the body. Piercing does not even achieve this; it lies on a further level where the beat of the music becomes completely dominant. The body has to be forcibly regulated. Anyone who goes to a house music club is really visiting a temple. The experience is so all-consuming that it becomes impossible to remain an observer. Either the visitor is sucked in, disappearing in the ecstatic experience or he moves on, more of an individual than ever before. Ironically, while dance was described only a generation ago as the vertical expression of a horizontal desire, it now requires a different definition beyond desire.

It is no coincidence that the modern generation divides into groups according to the music they opt for: punk, hard rock, house, rap, grunge, hardcore, techno, drum 'n' bass. It would be possible to do a study on the different methods of punctuating jouissance established by these different styles. These groups are all self-help groups, peer groups, that create their own rules and their own relationships, differing from those of the other groups. Above all, these rules determine how the body is used, especially one's own body. It is only when a sense of security and safety has been acquired that it is possible to make the transition to an other . . . *Order out of chaos.*

This last point brings us to the dimension of the law in the broad sense of ethical law, the way in which inter-relationships are arranged within a collectivity with regard to the distribution of pleasure. How does this law arise? What is it that must be regulated?

According to myth, the law is passed down from the mountain top and is given to imperfect beings ('Lord, I am not worthy to come to you'). Modern experience shows that the law is a group construction, made and controlled by a collectivity that at the same time determines individual identities and their interrelationships. Summarised in a general way, the law answers the following question: what may I and what can I use of the other person? It should not be forgotten that the person's own body is also an Other: I *have* a body, I am not a body. It is no coincidence that jouissance was originally a legal term, 'usufruct'.

If the law entails a regulation of jouissance via the group, what is the relationship between the law and desire? The answer that immediately springs to mind is that the law forbids desire—without the law my desire would no longer be desire, but would be translated into action. However, further reflection reveals a more complex relationship and gives rise to a curious question. Does the law forbid desire, or is desire actually instituted by the law?

> 'What follows? Is the Law identical with sin? Of course not. But except through law I should never have become acquainted with sin. For example, I should never have known what it was to covet, if the law had not said 'Thou shalt not covet.' Through that commandment sin found its opportunity, and produced in me all kinds of wrong desires. In the absence of law, sin is a dead thing.'

Lacan took this text from St Paul's *Epistle to the Romans* to reveal the complex relationship between these two elements. Without prohibition, there is no desire. Experience has often shown that when something is always permitted and always available, no one wants it. When the weather is fine every day, there is no such thing as good weather.

Conversely, anything that is forbidden and scarce automatically becomes desirable.

The consequences of this link between the law and desire are very far-reaching. What should we do about the idea of a 'policy of tolerance' with regard to any aspect of pleasurable experience, when it is predictable that this policy: (a) makes what is tolerated less attractive, precisely because it is permitted; (b) shifts the boundary of what is desirable onto the next prohibition, to what is not yet tolerated? There is no simple answer to these questions, and they require an ethical and therefore arbitrary stance. However, independently of any position that is adopted, it is predictable that a naïve form of liberalism will always carry within it the seeds of its own failure. It is no coincidence that the majority of the peer groups discussed above are working on the development of group norms that are anything but a policy of tolerance. This does not apply solely to the straight-edgers and Alcoholics Anonymous groups. Recent research has shown that the present generation of young people are quite determined to bring up their children much more strictly in the future than they were themselves.

The law does not prohibit desire; it actually brings it to life, together with its object. The actual target of the law is what lies beyond desire—jouissance. The real question then is not so much, what can I and what may I desire, but rather, how far can I go with jouissance? It is the same question that we raised earlier with regard to ancient Greece. In this form, the question is rather vague and scarcely indicates what it is aiming at. My formulation is, how far can I go before I disappear and cease to exist as an ego myself? The passivity so feared by the Greeks can be interpreted as the disappearance of the ego.

The law creates desire and also, therefore, the related pleasure, each time of a particular and private nature. If the ankle must remain covered or French kissing is forbidden, the experience of transgression is indescribable. No one has less pleasure than the person who has already had everything. By introducing a particular prohibition, and therefore the related pleasure, the law protects against the ultimate transgression of the ultimate pleasure, in which the subject itself disappears or causes another to disappear—the distinction becomes rather vague.

The regulation, and therefore the creation, of desire can be seen as the first and most important restriction on symbiotic jouissance. The longer and the more we are concerned with desire, the further we remain removed from jouissance. In the process, we enjoy a limited and particular form of pleasure determined by the group to which we belong, in conformity with the rules introduced by this group.

This kind of regulation is always determined by the dominant discourse. Not so very long ago, eternal truths, divine law or natural law, held sway. Post-modern discourse has presented us with the following deconstructions: (a) educational-religious discourse defined the transgressor as a sinner, and the remedy consisted of confession and penance—which were, in turn, inevitably eroticised; (b) nineteenth-century medical-scientific discourse made transgressors into sick people, patients who required treatment, although it was not clear what this treatment should be; (c) psychiatry and psychology rebaptised these patients as mentally ill, neurotics or perverts. The fact that the same erotic element persists in the latter two discourses is clear from the Hippocratic oath, which explicitly forbids the therapist from using his patient for his own sexual pleasure.

Present-day post-modern discourse argues for tolerance. Anything goes, though only by agreement, and anyone who is not normal is considered paranormal. The normophile must accept the paraphile. The link with God or nature disappears, while the link with the group becomes explicit. 'Normophilia: a condition of being erotosexually in conformity with the standard as dictated by customary, religious, or legal authority' (Money 1988: 214). However, the experience with peer groups shows that this tolerance is an illusion—the prescriptions are fully developed and imposed. The main difference from the past lies in the diversity of the prescriptions, and that is all.

It is predictable that this diversity will result in all sorts of discussions in which each group will preach its own views. Beyond the often empty cant that is talked in this respect, there remains one central question. What drives me towards this transgression, beyond the point where I myself cease to exist?

The meaning of life—teleology

Questions about the origin of something and its purpose are always impossible questions. What is the origin of the universe? What is its goal? When these questions are applied to biology and anthropology, the doors are thrown wide open for all sorts of wild speculation and ideological and religious interpretations. This is the domain of teleology, the presumed goal of, and in, life.

This brings us to dangerous territory, where the scientist of today hardly dares to tread. In so far as he does so, his answer will usually be related to procreation. The goal of life is to live on, to pass on one's *own* genetic material.

This is why women are 'irresistibly' driven to become pregnant and men are similarly driven to spread their seed. The irresistible element lies in the fact that this aim often operates quite separately, and sometimes despite the individual, who is seen more as a vehicle with an unknown driver at the wheel.

It is striking that in this respect, western science corresponds perfectly to its predecessors, the western religions. They too promised eternal life, albeit in a different form. Death was followed by a heavenly hereafter, on condition that certain moral values had been observed in earthly existence, conditions that inevitably amounted to restrictions on happiness and pleasure during life itself. Happiness was defined very clearly, because it was concerned not simply with being happy, but mainly with everything related to pleasure.

This last aspect reveals another correspondence between western religion and science. Nowadays, science also imposes the same sorts of conditions. The more unhealthy the life we lead, the shorter it is likely to be, and the smaller the chance of eternal life, in this case seen as reproduction. Like religious 'health', the scientific interpretation of 'healthier' is always related to giving up pleasure. As Frédéric Declercq remarked: 'Coffee without caffeine, wine without alcohol, cigarettes without nicotine, cakes without sugar'—I would just like to add telephone sex to this list . . . Soon this same science will be able to remove a minor imperfection from the way in which this elevated goal—eternal life—is achieved nowadays, namely the annoying fact that our children are not perfect replicas of ourselves. Attempts to keep ourselves alive in the deep freeze are only the first steps. We can now go one better, and in a short while I'll be able to clone my precious body and raise a carbon copy of myself. In this way, I'll undoubtedly avoid the mistakes made by my parents. The Oedipus complex is taking a bizarre turn. Oedipus meets Narcissus in Silicon Valley. The *Narcissipus* complex has a future.

Western science and religion are two hands on the womb pregnant with itself.

Viewed in this light, Freud's definition of the goal of life is quite different and sounds fairly minimalist or even nega-tive—the aim of achieving the lowest possible level of ten-sion. The fact that he considered this as an effect of what he called the 'pleasure principle' makes it even more curi-ous. In his first theory, pleasure is a complete absence of tension, while unpleasure is the opposite. For him the establishment of this goal is the effect of the drive itself, which is always aimed at wanting to return to an original state. The motto of any drive could be: 'It was better in the past', and the original past condition amounts to a zero level of tension. Freud wrote this during his laboratory period, inspired by the experimental psychology of his time. There was very little sexuality and reproduction in this view of things, and total pleasure was a sort of nir-vana.

The term 'nirvana' is not accidental. The ultimate zero level of tension is nothingness, the situation preceding life. In the context of eastern religion and philosophy, at first sight this seems a very surprising goal for a westerner. The goal of life is death, interpreted as definitive death and a liberation from the spiral of reincarnations. In the east the same toll must also be paid in life for this liberation—a moral toll that amounts to a restriction on pleasure.

It is not my intention to present semi-understood east-ern wisdom as a solution for western concerns. The wise men may have come from the east, but the grass is just as green here. However, such a view does allow us to relativise the self-evident nature of 'eternal life' as a western goal, and it also offers a quite unexpected link to death.

Since Philippe Ariès' study, *The Hour of Our Death* , it is clear how frightened we have become of dying. Today a 'beautiful' death is a sudden one, preferably during sleep, without illness or pain, and therefore completely unannounced. Not so very long ago, such a death was the most feared and was known as 'the thief in the night'. A good death was a death that was anticipated, so that one had the time to make detailed plans and prepare for what was to come.

No wonder that there is so little room today for the concept of a death drive. After all, a drive is surely concerned with sexuality and is therefore focused on life. The combination of these two terms, death and drive, is therefore impossible and even inconceivable. When Freud first put forward the idea in 1920, he immediately encountered opposition. Even within his own ranks, it was never accepted and was usually rejected as the product of an old man dying of cancer, who saw the end in sight. For the sake of completeness, we should add that his theory is very unclear on this point and has actually not been worked out very well. After Freud, the death drive was soon interpreted as a sort of internalised aggressive tendency or instinct that might play a role, for example, in suicide. In his ethological study on aggression, Konrad Lorenz quite rightly dismissed this, and since then the whole concept seems to be dead and buried.

'Doctor, if I stop drinking alcohol altogether, become a vegetarian and no longer go with women, will I live longer?

191

-' I can't tell you with any certainty whether you'll live any longer, but one thing I do know: it'll certainly seem much longer!'

A scientist wanted to study why some people lived much longer than others. When he visited an old people's home, he interviewed a number of the residents. One seventy-year-old assured him that he owed his age exclusively to a macrobiotic diet, an eighty-year-old added running the marathon, while a ninety-year-old declared that he had never looked at women. At that moment the astute gerontologist saw a perfect subject for his study stumbling past: he looked at least a hundred. The researcher turned to him, and asked whether he had also looked after his diet:

-'Yes, I always ate the best food, a lot of meat, the finest pastries, the best cream sauces.'

- 'And what about drinking? Did you keep an eye on that?'

-' I certainly did, I was very fussy about that! With a good meal you must have good wine, so I never accepted less than a grand cru, and my daily bottle of whisky is still a real malt. I don't like all these blends, they're pure poison.'

- 'And what about women?'

-' Don't talk to me about them. I used to do it at least twice a day, but this past year it hasn't been quite so easy.'

-' And yet you have reached such an old age. How on earth did you manage it?'

- 'Well you shouldn't exaggerate. After all, twenty-seven isn't really that old, is it?'

As long as we can laugh, we are healthy. The fact that the link between excessive sex and an early death has not been proved in any way does not detract from the popular sentiment expressed in these jokes. It is the conviction itself that deserves attention, not the content. This conviction reveals the link between death and sex and in a wider sense, between death and pleasure.

Sexuality implies death. Not because the life energy, which is presumed to be finite, is being pumped away with every orgasm, but because I am a sexuated creature. *Sexuated* means biologically differentiated whether toward the male side or toward the female side. This differentiation developed long ago during the evolution of life and introduced an entirely new life form with many more creative possibilities in 'the survival of the fittest'. After all, every generation always provided something new, another unique creation. The other, older possibility was the non-sexual life form in which sexually undifferentiated organisms were able to replicate themselves almost perfectly, either by cell division or as parasites on other organisms. However, there was a price to pay for the advantage of this new life form: every unique individual must eventually die. Sex and death stand on the same page of creation.

Our understanding fails at this point, which is in itself enough to evoke anxiety. The plain facts are fairly simple. Creatures that reproduce *asexually*—single-cell organisms, bacteria, viruses, prions, and in the near future, clones—in principle have eternal life, because they merely repeat themselves when they reproduce. Death is an accidental phenomenon and not at all necessary. Creatures that reproduce *sexually* must die: death is structurally built in to the design.[4] The one very particular cell division that characterises this life form, meiosis, results not only in the loss of half of the genetic material, but also, clearly, in the loss of the basic possibility for the individual to have eternal life. The chip that governs the programme contains the instruction to self-destruct after a while.

In this sense, every sexual drive, Eros, is from the very beginning intrinsically also a death drive, Thanatos. The two forms are the indistinguishable upper and lower side of a Moebius strip.[5] This brings us to Freud's last theory on drives.

Eros versus Thanatos

In the first essay, I emphasised the partial and auto-erotic nature of the drive, which can be interpreted as its operational characteristics. The Freudian opposition between Eros and Thanatos, the life and death drives, concerns the ultimate goal inherent in the impulse. The drive is aimed at the return to an original condition, that of the zero level of tension. Men did not have to wait for Freud to compare orgasm with a small death, 'la petite mort'. However, this does not prevent them from always striving for it. At the same time, there is an opposing force at work, another drive aimed at maintaining life and increasing tension. This avoids the small death and opts for a different form of pleasure.

The question is: who or what dies, to whom or to what do we return? Who or what wants to go on living, and does this also entail a return?

The terms 'life drive' and 'death drive' create the wrong impression. Eros and Thanatos are better, because they force us to devote more attention to the meaning we attach to these concepts. Eros has elements of fusion, amalgamation, the interconnection of disparate elements to form a larger entity, the fusion in which separate entities cease to exist. Thanatos is the fragmentation, the explosion, the bursting apart of an entity, the big bang, in which the accumulated force and tension are released and used up.

Freud stops at this point and does not discuss the idea any further. A closer inspection reveals that within this argument, the idea of life and death is extremely relative. Thanatos is the death of Eros—the Thanatos drive destroys the unity and causes the greater whole to fall apart into separate elements. Eros is the death of Thanatos—the Eros drive destroys the separate elements by fusing them in one entity. The two drives keep each other going by alternating endlessly. The time perspective is circular, not linear. Isis and Dionysus/Bacchus die and are constantly reborn.

In this sense, it is not so much a matter of the contrast between life and death, as Freud thought, but of the contrast between two different forms of life. On the one hand, there is life as an individual, as a separate and limited being with a clearly finite nature; on the other hand, there is life beyond this as part of a larger whole that continues to exist far beyond the individual. A honey bee has a life as an individual creature, with its own characteristics, tasks and possibilities. It dies after only six weeks in summer, but the swarm lives on with its own life, a different life from that of the ephemeral individual. Some entomologists still discuss the question of how they should study this *apis mellifera*: as a 'nation', that is, as a group, or as an individual. The latter can never exist separately from the group, but obviously the converse equally applies.

This difference between two interpretations of the word 'life' is expressed fairly clearly in ancient Greek, where a distinction is made between *bios and zoë*. Zoë—as in zoology—is indestructible and therefore eternal life, the all-embracing source and endpoint of all things. *Bios*—as in biology—is the individual, more limited manifestation of this eternal life which returns to the *zoë* once it has come to an end. The whole process is seen as circular, a constantly alternating cycle that the Greeks also saw in the seasons, in day and night and in astrology.

As a working principle, in the sense of Aristotle's Prime Mover, this link between Eros and Thanatos easily transcends the relationship between man and woman, though this does not mean that the human couple is not subordinated to it—far from it.[6]

Eros is the rosy side of the relationship, the erotic aspect focused on fusion, a fusion that goes far beyond the coupling of the sexual act because it is aimed at the original symbiosis with the mother, and beyond this, on the symbiosis with the life that was lost when the ego was created as an ego. It is no coincidence that it is always the man who is driven towards the woman. He is the one who fell away, was left behind and who irresistibly returns to his place of origin. The price for this is having to give up the result of this creation. The ego must disappear as an ego, if the symbiosis with the Other is to succeed. Beyond this, the symbiotic unit must also disappear into the even wider life, *zoë*, that lies behind it and that is ineffable. Is it surprising then, that a subject on his journey falls prey to anxiety, and draws back from a jouissance that both fuels and consumes him?

This is where the other aspect comes into play: Thanatos, which is responsible for the two-backed beast falling apart, letting the Other go with the orgasmic grimaces of phallic pleasure, so that the previously experienced fusion bursts apart and the I returns to its biosphere. Afterwards, each of us feels more of an individual than before, but also very alone and sometimes rather sad. Until we begin again, *encore*, throughout life, far beyond the actual possibilities of reproduction, just in order to get 'there'. And we do get there. In the end.

Eros and Thanatos are not separate drives: they indicate opposing directions for the course of life. This accounts for a typical characteristic—the more one of the two directions is present and predominates, the stronger the other will become as well. This does not only apply to couples. The more a united Europe is achieved, the stronger nationalist and even regionalist trends become. Conversely, fragmentation leads to coalition. When the wider social group falls apart, this always results in the establishment of all sorts of subgroups and subcultures. The death of marriage has made the couple more important than ever before.

I will leave the way in which this applies in a general sense, from geopolitics to cosmology, to the expert reader. In the sexual relationship I can draw a line and indicate the direction in which things are moving. This line lies between the man and the woman in a direction from the man to the woman, or the other way round, away from the woman. Eros is the name for the first direction, Thanatos for the second. Each of the directions seems to have its own sex, its own pleasure and its own affect; woman, jouissance and anxiety are part of Eros; man, phallic pleasure and sadness are part of Thanatos. The affect indicates the break where pleasure results in too great a loss: anxiety relates to the disappearance of the ego that is a condition for jouissance. Sadness relates to the loss of symbiosis as a result of phallic pleasure. In this respect, the opposition between man and woman is extremely relative and should be interpreted more as an active versus a passive position, which any subject can adopt vis-à-vis the other.

This explains why sexuality, no matter how satisfying it may be, always contains the seeds of dissatisfaction—the pleasure of one direction detracts from that of the other tendency. Freud anticipated this when he wrote in 1896 that sexuality itself contained a source of displeasure.

The two directions are clearly sex-related. Eros and jouissance belong on the side of the woman, Thanatos and phallic pleasure on the side of the man. Each has within itself the potential, or even the aspiration, for the other. The female orgasm is also phallic—she is even multi-orgasmic. However, she needs it less and does not feel it to be essential. Sometimes it can even diminish her potential for gaining pleasure from the other, the lasting aspect of symbiosis in which the original bond is restored. The man is all too familiar with jouissance and is constantly seeking it, though he also flees from it in the short-circuiting of his phallic pleasure, because this other enjoyment turns him into an object without a will, part of a larger whole.

Both frigidity and premature ejaculation amount to a refusal of the other direction.

This sex-relatedness assigns roles, despite patriarchal systems and emancipation movements. The woman represents symbiosis, the alma mater. She is there and does not have to do much except wait. The man was once part of her, is actually no more than her product and will return sooner or later, in any case. He is driven towards her womb, full of desire and aggression at the same time. According to Freud, there are three women in every man's life: the woman who bears him, the woman who takes him in, and the woman who destroys him. All three are mothers: his own mother, the mother of his children and mother earth who takes him back.

The drive, as a liminal factor between the psychological and the somatic, is always looking for a psychic representation, an image, an anchor that will provide support. Without this, it will continue to turn round and round in the no man's land between the body and the mind, careering and then spinning out of control, until there is an explosion. The drive is a measure of the work demanded of the psyche.

This anchoring onto a representation (image or word), amounts to the always impossible leap from drive to desire. It is impossible because the two are radically different, and in this leap there must be a metamorphosis so that the process is more like a hop-step-jump. On the other side of the barrier, the Other is waiting as a subject, while the drive needs only some of this Other, only part of it, something that takes the place of something that can never be again.

The common response is one of disappointment. *That* isn't it; he/she is not the right one. Some people continue to seek feverishly for this something right up to the end, hoping against hope to find it, rather like a child breaking up his toys so that he can find 'it' inside. The toy is broken and he has found nothing.

This form of transgression results in destructive jouissance. Few people go this far, because the barriers of anxiety are too great. In this respect, emergency psychiatry has been very instructive, at least for anyone who is prepared to listen. Many patients who have been suddenly admitted with an attack resembling a psychosis appear to have crossed this boundary. The majority remain on the safe side and stop on the way at the point where the jouissance remains controllable. As the final stop on the trajectory, this point necessarily has a somewhat repetitive and therefore monotonous character, which is fatal for passion. It becomes a ritual, almost comparable to an incantatory ritual performed to exorcise something unknown, out there.

Beyond this, there is sometimes another possibility. The way in which the drive and desire appear in a couple is partly determined by the group and partly by the two subjects involved. The relationship is premeditated and prescribed, but premeditation can turn into meditation, prescription into creative writing. The results can never be generalised, but by their very nature will always be very different. Instead of being reduced to a category ('the' man and 'the' woman) and the related repetition, the whole emphasis is now on the difference. For Lacan (1963), love is the only thing that can ensure the link between drive and desire—'*Seul l'amour permet à la jouissance de condescendre au désir*' (Only love allows jouissance to condescend to desire).

This means that a sexual relationship between a man and a woman becomes the sublimation of the impossible sexual relationship between man and woman.

. . . and to conclude:

It was a philosophical exercise, with the aim of discovering to what extent thinking about your own history can liberate you from thinking your silent thoughts and can provide an opportunity to think differently. (Foucault, *The History of Sexuality*, Vol. 2, my translation)

Notes

I. *The Impossible Couple*

[1] In terms of political correctness, I should probably write consistently 'he or she' and 'human being' for 'man'. Similarly I should remind the reader each time I use the word 'couple' that I am referring to homo- as well as heterosexual couples. Such a style results either in a reversed racism (Man is the nigger of the world) or in an obsessional superego spiral. Both of these miss the crux of the matter. Each couple elaborates a relationship between active and passive, *independently of whatever gender this couple may have*. As far as I am concerned, this is much more important and cannot be addressed by politically correct expressions. Since this theme will be elaborated throughout the book, I must ask for some patience. In order to reassure the politically correct reader—for me, the original couple is not male/female but child/first caretaker. This is closely associated to the relationship between the body and its own subjectivity, and changes the whole picture.

[2] A homosexual colleague and friend informed me that 'heterosexuals start their erotic career searching for and finding their great love and end it a decade later looking for pure sex, whilst homosexuals start with enjoying pure sex and end with love'. Maybe Plato was right after all . . . (See parts 191 d and e of the *Symposium* [Plato 1998]).

[3] It can be argued that childhood as such is an invention of western culture during the last two centuries, starting with Rousseau's *Emile* through to Dr. Spock. This is beautifully demonstrated by Philippe Ariès in *Centuries of Childhood*. As far as the 'eternal' aspect of mother and child is concerned, I wish to stress the fact that our contemporary form is indeed contemporary, as has been demonstrated by Elisabeth Badinter in *The Myth of Motherhood*. So what is 'eternal' about this aspect of love between mother and child? What I am referring to here is the primal dual, symbiotic relationship between the infant and the mother that evokes Plato's original double human being. The denomination, interpretation and elaboration of this relationship as 'love' is an effect peculiar to individual cultures.

[4] This is undoubtedly the best known quotation from his study on repetition. The lengthier quote is as follows: 'Hope is a charming maiden that slips through the fingers, recollection is a beautiful old woman but of no use at the instant, repetition is a beloved wife of whom one never tires' (Kierkegaard 1964).

[5] Aristophanes' fable is fascinating in itself, not only because of its 'political correctness' *avant la lettre*. If one reads the whole story, it becomes obvious that genital sex enters the picture only at a *secondary* stage, and is absent from the first part. Indeed, once the original double being was bisected, each half

was perpetually searching for its corresponding half, but not, as we might expect, for the purpose of having sex. 'Now, when the work of bisection was complete, it left each half with a desperate yearning for the other, and they ran together and flung their arms around each other's necks, and asked for nothing better than to be rolled into one. So much so, that they began to die of hunger and general inertia, for neither would do anything without the other' (Plato 1998: 543–4). Zeus took pity on them and introduced yet another change to their bodies: he moved their reproductive organs to the front (originally they were placed on the outer side of the body), thus making sexual intercourse possible (previously reproduction had taken place via external fertilisation). This change, particularly the ensuing possibility for genital union, temporarily set the human being free from its longing and made it possible for it to turn to the activities necessary for survival.

The beauty of this fable is that the transition thus described is not from a 'rounded whole' to a bisection into a male and female differentiation, but from a rounded whole into two parts (whatever the gender) longing for each other totally and rendering all other considerations unimportant. The *genital* interest enters the scene at a later stage and turns the original total process into a partial one because of the lethal nature of this first process.

Both gender and genital sex are a secondary although necessary issue, following a primary relationship within a global union—that's Plato's message.

[6] 'Dark continent' is the metaphor that Freud used to describe the psychology of the woman. He meant the unknown, but the actual effect of Freudian psychoanalysis on women was indeed a kind of colonisation at first, with all the classic consequences, such as the imposition of the coloniser's norms on the colonised. This was particularly clear in Freud's failure to theorise the female version of the Oedipus complex (Verhaeghe 1997: 205-240). Lacan tried to respond to this failure in Seminar XX, *Encore* (Lacan 1998). However, I am not sure that this problem has been sufficiently thought through in contemporary Lacanian psychoanalysis.

[7] This is what the analyst means by what, at first sight, seems a very curious view, namely that the *other* person functions as *my* 'phallus' in this sort of relationship. The word phallus is misleading here, because it tends to make one think in anatomical and biological terms. Actually, in this line of reasoning, the phallus serves as a symbol—a signifier—for what both sexes can never have enough, (the man) or can never be enough (the woman) in meeting the needs of the other person. This is where they start to look for 'it' from the other person, convinced that he/she will have 'it'.

II. *Fathers in Flight*

1 The most recent illustration of this comes from the USA, where—following the latest school shooting at Columbine High School, Colorado—the State of Colorado took the decision to connect each classroom, by direct telephone line, to the Police Station. Where authority disappears, it would seem, power enters the scene—well-armed. Similarly in Europe the cry for youth prisons has been increasing steadily over the years, especially in the so-called 'progressive' countries such as Scandinavia and the Netherlands.

2 Otto Weininger, a brilliant philosopher, Jew, and homosexual, published this work in 1903. In it he damned Jews and women in the same way—and then committed suicide.

3 Of course, these men might simply have been exceptions within their time to the general rule of patriarchy—after all, weren't their children neurotic? But on second thoughts, perhaps their 'exceptional' position wasn't all that exceptional after all, but simply the reverse side of the patriarchal coin. Patriarchy—especially in its excessive forms—*hides* masculine anxiety and dependence. The less the anxiety, the less the defensive stance of patriarchy is required. These men were—respectively—the fathers of the Rat Man, the Wolf Man, and Dora (Freud 1909b, 1918, 1905a). The father of Little Hans (Freud 1909a) was utterly dominated by his wife.

4 The creation of meaning always goes back to a *creatio ex nihilo*, since there is no predetermined meaning as such. The consequences of this thesis are far-reaching. There is an implication that the core of the discussion does not reside in the first instance with the father figure—he is merely the sociocultural support for something more important—the symbolic system which turns a human being into a human subject. Therefore, the discussion should be re-centred on what Lacan, following Freud, considers to be the basis of this symbolic system: the phallus in its dimension of radical signifier. To my knowledge, Zizek is the most intelligent commentator on this debate since, in his *Metastases of Enjoyment* (pp. 201-203), he emphasises the necessarily *empty* or *negative* character of the phallic signifier. If we agree with Zizek, it can be said that those who criticise Freud and Lacan for their supposedly patriarchal stance, are the same people who endorse it since they fail to see the radical innovation in Lacanian theory.

5 *La Volonté de Savoir* ('The Will to Knowledge') is the title of Volume 1 of Foucault's *The History of Sexuality* (Foucault 1990). Unaccountably, some English translations omit the subtitle of Volume 1 altogether.

III. *The Drive*

[1] 'In my opinion there must be an independent source for the release of unpleasure in sexual life: once that source is present, it can activate sensations of disgust, lend force to morality, and so on' (Freud 1985: 164). This idea of an independent source of unpleasure in sexual life stands in direct contrast to his previous ideas, as elaborated—for example—in 'On "Civilized" Sexual Morality and Modern Nervous Illness' (1908). It took him another twenty years to work this out more fully but, when he finally did, no-one took him seriously. As we will see, this concerns his final theory of the drive, of an internal antagonism between Eros and the death drive—in other words, the antagonism between two totally different kinds of pleasure.

[2] In contrast to traumatic neurosis, the proportion of actually occurring traumas is fairly small in hysteria, and is expressed differently in terms of symptoms. Specifically in terms of self-mutilation this difference is very striking. A traumatic self-mutilation takes place on the level of jouissance, a hysterical self-mutilation on the level of desire. The latter implies, of course, identification—which is why hysterical auto-mutilation belongs to the cultural scene and is always provocative. In this sense, Renata Salecl (1998) is right in recognising hysterical auto-mutilation as a post-modern attempt to belong to a certain group—that is, to acquire an identity through a signifier written on the body. However, hysterical auto-mutilation should not be confused with post-traumatic auto-mutilation, which is not very clear in her paper. The same difference can be recognised between hysterical anorexia nervosa (as a cultural identificatory phenomenon) and anorexia nervosa as such. The first didn't exist during the time of the fully fleshed bodies of Rubens; and the second is independent of such cultural shifts. On the other hand, the very fact that hysteria is producing cultural variants on bodily mutilation says a lot about our actual culture. Hysteria always magnifies underlying processes. In this case, the hysterical subject is demonstrating the traumatic underside of contemporary culture. We are living in the era of the drive. I have elaborate upon this theme elsewhere (Verhaeghe 1998b), and so I won't go into it any further here.

[3] *The Use of Pleasure* is also the title of Volume 2 of Foucault's *The History of Sexuality* (1988).

[4] This gives a whole new meaning to the old Freudian idea that 'anatomy is destiny', although anatomy must be replaced by 'sexual reproductivity'. As an idea it has far-reaching consequences, because it assumes a basic duality at the birth of human life. This is very difficult to understand, for a number

of reasons. During a private discussion with Joan Copjec (March 1999) I argued that gender is a secondary construction, a mere effect of the Other, but this does not imply that Lacanian psychoanalysis takes a Butlerian stance. This secondary construction is based on a determining duality which does not concern the body (the body is an effect of discourse) but which has everything to do with the *organism*. This term is used explicitly by Lacan in his Seminar XI (Lacan 1991a). Denominating this original duality as 'male' and 'female' is—from my point of view—a retroactive interpretation of a more fundamental and original division. ('In man, however, this relation to nature is altered by a certain dehiscence at the heart of the organism, a primordial Discord' [Lacan 1977: 4]). Its essence is not this division in itself, but the fact that something is lost, and that life tries to regain it, although in such a way that time and again, the loss is reconfirmed. That is why Lacan speaks of a circular but non-reciprocal structure, resulting in an ever-missed encounter. The best known example of this is the (non-)relationship between man and woman, but this is only its very last implementation, which demonstrates the same failure as its previous implementations. See note 6.

5 Moebius strip—take a strip of paper at least 30cm long; hold one end in each hand, make a turn of 180° and bring the ends together. Then stick the two ends together neatly with tape. Now try to show which is the upper and lower side of the strip obtained in this way. Art lovers merely have to look at Escher's etchings.

6 Gender identity is the final implementation of an original division, and contains the same structurally determined failure when it attempts to undo this division. Based on Seminar XI (Lacan 1991a) and later Lacanian theory, I recognise here several forms of what Lacan calls a homologous structure between organism and subject. The first is the 'advent of living'. The advent of sexually differentiated life-forms implies the loss of eternal life; the attempt to return takes place through sexual reproduction, which confirms the original loss. The second is the 'advent of the I', implying the loss of the being. The third is the 'advent of the subject', implying the loss of the I as master of itself; the attempt to regain this mastery takes place through signifiers, which confirm the original loss and division. In this advent of the subject, gender identity is installed through the signifiers of the Other, as the last form of alienation. As I argued elsewhere, the net result of this is that man is not so much a divided subject but more a quartered being (Verhaeghe 1999b).

Bibliography

Aeschylus (1993) *The Oresteia*, trans. H. Lloyd-Jones, Berkeley: University of California Press.

Ariès, P. (1962) *Centuries of Childhood*, London: Cape.

Ariès, P. (1985)*The Hour of Our Death*, trans. J. Lloyd, Cambridge MA: Harvard University Press.

Armstrong, K. (1999) *The History of God: The 4000 Year Quest of Judaism, Christianity and Islam*, London:Vintage.

Auster, P. (1982) *The Invention of Solitude*, London & Boston: Faber & Faber.

Badinter, E. (1981) *The Myth of Motherhood: an Historical View of the Maternal Instinct*, London: Souvenir Press.

Bellow, S. (1984) *Henderson, the Rain King*, London: Penguin.

Borges, J. L. (1967) *The Book of Imaginary Beings*, trans. N. Di Giovanni, London: Penguin.

Burgess, A. (1986) *Little Wilson and Big God*, New York: Grove Weidenfeld.

Copjec, J. (1995), *Read my Desire: Lacan Against the Historicists*, Cambridge, Mass.: MIT.

Conrad, J. (1996) *Heart of Darkness*, Boston: Bedford Books.

De Rougemont, D. (1929) *Love in the Western World*, trans. M. Belgion, New York: Doubleday.

Declercq, F. (1997) *Het Reële van de pulsie als raamwerk voor de prognose van de psychoanalytische kuur. Lacans fundering van Freuds ontdekking*, doctoral thesis, University of Ghent.

Elias, N. (1982) *The Civilizing Process: Sociogenetic and Psychogenetic Investigations*, Oxford: Blackwell.

Euripides (1954) *The Bacchae and Other Plays*, trans. P. Vellacott, London: Penguin.

Ferenczi, S. (1955) 'Confusion of Tongues Between Adults and the Child' in *Final Contributions to the Problems and Methods of Psycho-Analysis*, trans. J. Dupont, London: Hogarth.

Foucault, M. (1988) *The History of Sexuality, Vol. 2: The Use of Pleasure*, trans. R. Hurley, London: Penguin.

Foucault, M. (1990) *The History of Sexuality, Vol. 1: The Will to Truth*, trans. R. Hurley, London: Penguin.

French, M. (1995) *Women's History of the World*, Maryland: Ballantine.

Freud, S. (1905a) 'Fragment of an Analysis of a Case of Hysteria', S.E. VII: 1-122, London: Hogarth.

Freud, S. (1905b)*Three Essays on the Theory of Sexuality*, S. E. VII: 123-245, London: Hogarth.

Freud, S. (1908) '"Civilized" Sexual Morality and Modern Nervous Illness', S.E. IX: 177-204, London: Hogarth.

Freud, S. (1909a) 'Analysis of a Phobia in a Five-Year-Old Boy', S.E. X: 1-149, London: Hogarth.

Freud, S. (1909b) 'Notes Upon a Case of Obsessional Neurosis', S.E. X: 151:249, London: Hogarth.

Freud, S. (1915) 'Instincts and Their Vicissitudes', S.E. XIV: 109-140, London: Hogarth.

Freud, S. (1918) 'From the History of an Infantile Neurosis', S.E. XVII: 1-122, London: Hogarth.

Freud, S. (1931) 'Female Sexuality', S.E. XXI: 221-243, London: Hogarth.

Freud, S. (1913) *Totem and Taboo*, S.E. XIII: 1-161, London: Hogarth.

Freud, S. (1939) *Moses and Monotheism*, S.E. XXIII: 1-137, London: Hogarth.

Freud, S., with Breuer, J. (1895) *Studies on Hysteria,*, S.E. II, London: Hogarth.

Freud, S. (1985) *The Complete Letters of Sigmund Freud to Wilhelm Fliess 1887-1904*, trans. and ed. by J. Masson,

Cambridge MA & London: Belknap Press of Harvard University.

Graves, R. (1997) *The White Goddess*, London: Faber & Faber.

Greer, G. (1971) *The Female Eunuch*, London: Flamingo; New York: McGraw-Hill.

Greer, G. (1999) *The Whole Woman*, London: Doubleday.

Hadewijch, (1980) *The Complete Works*, New York: Paulist Press.

Herman, J.L. (1998) *Trauma and Recovery: From Domestic Abuse to Political Terror*, London: Rivers Oram Press.

Huizinga, J. *The Waning of the Middle Ages: A Study of the Forms of Life, Thought and Art in France and the Netherlands in the XIVth and XVth Centuries*, New York: Doubleday.

Israël, L. (1976) *L'hysterique, le sexe et le médecin*, Paris: Masson.

Kaplan, H. S. (1994) *Disorders of Sexual Desire and Other New Concepts and Techniques in Sex Therapy*, New York: Brunner Mazel.

Kierkegaard, S. (1964) *Repetitions: an Essay in Experimental Psychology*, trans. W. Lowrie, New York: Harper.

Lacan, J. (1962-63) *Seminar X: l'angoisse* (unpublished).

Lacan, J. (1991a) *Seminar XI, The Four Fundamental Concepts of Psycho-analysis*, ed. J.-A. Miller, trans. A. Sheridan, London: Penguin.

Lacan, J. (1991b) *Le Séminaire, livre XVII: L'Envers de la Psychanalyse*, ed. J.-A. Miller, Paris: Seuil.

Lacan, J. (1998) *Seminar XX, Encore: On Female Sexuality, The Limits of Love and Knowledge*, trans. B. Fink, New York/London: Norton.

Lessing, D. (1966-7) *Children of Violence*, four volumes, London: Panther.

Lessing, D. (1995) *Under My Skin*, London: Flamingo.

Lévi-Strauss, C. (1992) *The Elementary Structures of Kinship*, trans. J. Harle Bell, Boston: Beacon Press.

Lorenz, K. (1997) *On Aggression*, trans. M. Latzke, New York: Fine Communications.

Masters, W., & Johnson, V. (1966) *Human Sexual Response*, Boston: Little Brown.

Miles, R. (1988) *The Women's History of the World*, London: Harper Collins.

Milgram, S. (1965) 'Some Conditions of Obedience and Disobedience to Authority' in Human Relations, 1965, 18, 51-75.

Money, J. (1988) *Gay, Straight and In-Between: The Sexuology of Erotic Orientation*, Oxford: OUP.

Nin, A. (1977) *Delta of Venus*, London: Penguin.

Ovid (1998) *Metamorphoses*, ed. E.J. Kenney, trans. A.D. Melville, Oxford: OUP.

Paglia, C. (1990) *Sexual Personae: Art and Decadence From Nefertiti to Emily Dickinson*, London: Penguin; New York: Vintage.

Plato (1994) *The Collected Dialogues, including the Letters*, edited by E. Hamilton and H. Cairns, Bollingen Series LXXI, Princeton: Princeton UP.

Prigogine, I., & Stengers, I. (1985) *Order out of Chaos: Man's New Dialogue with Nature*, London: Flamingo / Fontana.

Reed, E. (1975) *Woman's Evolution: From Matriarchal Clan to Patriarchal Family*, New York: Pathfinder Press.

Salecl, R. (1998) *(Per)Versions of Love and Hate*, London & New York: Verso.

Sloterdijk, P. (1997) *Critique of Cynical Reason*, Minneapolis: University of Minnesota.

Sophocles (1993) *Oedipus Rex*, trans. R.D. Dawe, Cambridge: Cambridge University Press.

Steinbeck, J. (1977) *The Grapes of Wrath*, New York: Viking.

Stevenson, R. L. (1985) *Dr Jekyll and Mr Hyde*, New York: Bantam.

Theweleit, K. (1987) *Male Fantasies Vol. 1 Women, Floods, Bodies, History*, trans. S. Conway, Minneapolis: University of Minnesota; London: Polity.

Theweleit, K. (1989) *Male Fantasies Vol. 2 Male Bodies: Psychoanalyzing the White Terror*, trans. C. Turner & E. Carter, Minneapolis: University of Minnesota; London: Polity.

Tuchman, B. (1987) *The Proud Tower: A Portrait of the World Before the War, 1890-1914*, London: Papermac.

Vandenberg, J. (1962) *Metabletica ou la psychologie historique*, Paris: Buchet.

Verhaeghe, P. (1995) 'From impossibility to inability: Lacan's theory on the four discourses', *The Letter* 3: 76-100.

Verhaeghe, P. (1997) *Does the Woman Exist? From Freud's Hysteric to Lacan's Feminine*, London/New York: Rebus/Other Press.

Verhaeghe, P. (1998a) 'On the Lacanian Subject: Causation and Destitution of a Pre-ontological Non-entity', in *Key Concepts of Lacanian Psychoanalysis*, ed. D. Nobus, London: Rebus Press.

Verhaeghe, P. (1998b) 'Trauma and hysteria within Freud and Lacan', *The Letter* 14: 87-105.

Verhaeghe, P. (1999a) 'The collapse of the function of the father and its effect on gender roles', *Journal for the Psychoanalysis of Culture and Society* 4, 1: 18-30.

Weininger, O. (1906) *Sex and Character*, London: Heinemann.

Zizek, S. (1994) *The Metastases of Enjoyment: Six Essays on Woman and Causality*, London/New York: Verso.

Films

Apocalypse Now (USA, Francis Ford Coppola, 1979).
Beavis and Butthead (USA, Mike Judge, 1993).
Cabaret (USA, Bob Fosse, 1972).
The Crying Game (USA, Neil Jordan, 1992).
Easy Rider (USA, Denis Hopper, 1969)
Empire of the Senses/ L'empire du sens (Japan/France, Nagisa Oshima, 1976).
How to Irritate People (Great Britain, Monty Python, 1968).
Kramer v. Kramer (USA, Benton Robert, 1979)
Last Tango in Paris (Italy, Bernardo Bertolucci, 1972).
M. Butterfly (USA, David Cronenberg, 1993).
Man of Flowers (Australia, Paul Cox, 1983).
Monty Python's Life of Brian (Great Britain, Terry Jones, 1979).
Mrs. Doubtfire (USA, Chris Columbus, 1993).
9½Weeks (USA, Adrian Lyne, 1985).
Pleasantville (USA, Gary Ross 1999)
Shine (Great Britain/Australia, Scott Hicks, 1996).
The Simpsons (USA, Matt Groening, 1987).
South Park (USA, Trey Parker and Matthew Stone, 1997).
A Streetcar Named Desire (USA, Elia Kazan, 1952).
Tootsie (USA, Sydney Pollack, 1982).
Trainspotting (Great Britain, Danny Boyle,1997)
Ulee's Gold (USA,1997, Victor Nunez)